Dressage Insights

Dressage Insights

Excerpts from Experts

KATHY CONNELLY AND MARIETTA WHITTLESEY

Half Halt Press, Inc.
Boonsboro, Maryland

Dressage Insights: Excerpts from Experts

© 1994 Kathy Connelly & Marietta Whittlesey

Published in the United States of America by

Half Halt Press, Inc.
P.O. Box 67
Boonsboro, MD 21713

Photos by Terri Miller, except where otherwise noted.

Book and jacket design by Patrice Gallagher.

Printed in the United States of America.

Library of Congress Cataloging-in-Publication Data

Connelly, Kathy, 1950–
      Dressage insights : excerpts from experts / Kathy Connelly and
Marietta Whittlesey.
            p.   cm.
      Interviews with America's top dressage riders.
      ISBN 0-939481-38-3
      1. Dressage.   2. Dressage riders --Interviews.   3. Dressage--United
States. 4. Dressage riders--United States--Interviews.
I. Whittlesey, Marietta. II. Title.
IN PROCESS
798.2'3--dc20   94-36096
                                                                    CIP

Contents

Acknowledgments

To all of the riders and trainers included in this book, who made enormous contributions of time and knowledge for their original interview and then, thereafter, reviewed the reams of material so we could get it "just right." They truly reflected a generosity of spirit.

To my friend and coauthor, Marietta, who quite simply did a phenomenal job. She was a paragon on fastidiousness, and plowed through mountains of manuscripts to condense without losing the flavor or riders' thoughts or personalities.

I would also like to thank Beth Carnes, the mind behind Half Halt Press for her belief in this project, her support and extraordinary patience. And, a special thanks to Betsey Jansen, Carey Radtke, and Bernd Schopf for their time and ideas to this book. Their assistance was invaluable.

And lastly, to all of the horses of all of the people, riders and trainers contained herein, who brought us along by showing what more they needed to know, so we would keep learning.

> Kathy Connelly
> Harvard, Massachusetts
> May, 1994

Above all, I want to thank Kathy for her many hours of brilliant and precise teaching, and all her essential work in the planning, interviewing and writing of this book as well as for her unflagging friendship. In addition, there are a number of valiant others whose energy is contained herein. They are: Orlena Argall who made the initial introduction, Elvia Gignoux, editorial assistant, typist and groom extraordinaire, Rob Longley who carried on the word processing, Barbara Perkins who never forgot a detail and Joyce Hunt who cheerfully made every deadline. Special thanks go to Lynn Webb, without whose ability to handle chaos with grace I would have gone mad, and to Rebecca Fuller who helped so much in Florida. And of course to Addison Berkey, the best husband any rider/writer could dream of.

Marietta Whittlesey
Stanfordville, New York
June, 1994

Introduction

*T*his book is a montage of ideas collected over a period of two years from some of the leading dressage riders and trainers in the United States. Most previous dressage books presented one individual's viewpoint and ideas, and so it seemed an exciting prospect to put together a book with the combined wisdom and experience of an assemblage of successful and dedicated riders and trainers.

The interview process was a fascinating tour of each rider's mind and philosophy. The spectrum of ideology was infinite. Naturally, it would be impossible to capture and display all that any one person has learned on the subject of dressage, let alone a group of individuals. Each rider offered to share knowledge in his or her particular areas of interest. These conversations by no means reflect the full scope of their knowledge or experience. We felt that the magic of a book like this lay in capturing each individual's unique voice, and so we kept the excerpts as conversational as possible rather than editing them into uniformity. The book does not include all of the riders and trainers that we invited to participate. Many could not participate because of their individual time and schedule constraints.

Being a dressage rider in the United States is a challenge. Not only is ours an enormous country, but we are also thousands of miles from Europe, the recognized nucleus of international dressage. Our riders and trainers have made substantial sacrifices of time and expense for the privilege of training in Europe with the world's maestros. The results of these individuals' quests for the knowledge are contributing significantly to the improved quality of dressage in the United States. There is so much yet to learn.

Although styles of riding and approaches to training varied among the riders and trainers in this book, what was universal was an impressive commitment and dedication to learning the truth and improving themselves so that they could provide more clarity in their riding for their horses. Dressage, in French, means training, and is built upon the principles of classical horsemanship. It can be described as the harmonious development of the equine individual, both in his mental and physical capacities through the movements and levels of dressage until his inherent talent has been maximized. It is the job of the trainer to maintain the horse's naturalness, balance and elegance.

This requires great skill, time, consistency and patience as the horse develops strength, suppleness and obedience while simultaneously remaining free in his movement. The trainer/rider must be the horse's director, masseur, physical therapist, psychologist, strategist and cheerleader, all in one. That is challenge enough. Each time a new horse is mounted, the journey of learning begins anew.

Training horses in dressage is also the ongoing lifetime development of the human individual. To become a trainer and understand the complexities of the horse, the rider must learn about himself and be dedicated to his own mental and physical development. The trainer must discover, acknowledge and shed his defenses, obstinacy and arrogance. He must strive for personal integrity, humility and the desire to grow in order to maintain a truthful relationship with his horse.

The demands of growth require honesty, creativity, self-reflection, self-discipline and the coping mechanisms for dealing with intermittent failure and success. Trainers must learn what it means to do less to achieve more and to reward generously for what may be only a small achievement in order to maintain a horse's desire to try. After all, why should my friend continue giving me his poetry to read if all I do is correct his spelling?

The human race has been magnetically attracted to the horse throughout history. Consider the words of Xenophon in 400 B.C.: "A horse is such a thing of beauty, none will tire of looking at him." It is impossible to extinguish the passion we feel for our horses, their beauty and the development of their prowess. Additionally, there is a spiritual cathartic process when we combine our nature with theirs to share the risks and profits of the training process. Let us hope through more knowledge and more training, through kindness, or "gentling" as Xenophon referred to it, that not only will we exult in the development of our horses, but ultimately find the way to ourselves.

Each rider in this book, by sharing ideas, revealed his quest for the truth. That was the goal of this book. It is my hope that from these pages readers will find some answers along their journey to maintain the brightness of their horses' souls and their own.

Kathy Connelly

The Contributors

Gwen Blake

Gwen began competing the year she started riding, at the age of 12. She reached an "A" rating in the Pony Club. After spending two years training with Hilda Gurney, she now trains with Olympic veteran Robert Dover. Gwen has participated in USET training sessions with Harry Boldt, Robert Dover and Reiner Klimke. She has won 15 state championships in Training Level to Grand Prix competitions, and has won eight AHSA, Insilco and Miller's Championships in competitions ranging from Fourth Level to Grand Prix.

In 1991, Gwen won many competitions, including Intermediare I at CDA Venice, Prix St. Georges, at Wellington Winter Festival Dressage, CDI, Prix St. Georges, Intermediare I and Intermediare Freestyle, at Central Florida Classic, open Prix St. Georges, USET Festival of Champions, and Intermediare I at the Pan American Games Selection Class, USET Festival of Champions. She represented the United States at the Pan-American Games in Cuba that year and led the team to win the silver medal riding Juvel. Juvel was also the top representative for the Seoul Olympic Games in 1988. She is currently based in Washington State where she teaches students and trains young horses.

Photo on page 21.

Charlotte Bredahl

Charlotte has lived in California the past 15 years. Monsieur is the second horse she has trained to Grand Prix. She has also trained four other horses to Prix St. Georges.

In 1990 and 1991 Charlotte was third at the USET National Grand Prix finals. In 1991 she received a USET grant to train and compete in Europe for four months.

In 1992 she made the squad of six rider/horse combinations to train and compete in Europe prior to the Olympics. During shows in Europe she made the U.S. Team, a team that brought home the bronze medal.

She is currently bringing another horse along, seven year old Lugano, who will compete at Prix St. Georges this summer.

Photo on page 25.

Kathy Connelly

At 19, Kathy rode in her first international competition representing the USPC "A" Three Day Event Team in Australia. In 1988, Kathy was the Miller's USET United States Grand Prix Freestyle Champion and was short listed for the 1988 Olympic Games. She was the 1989 United States Grand Prix World Cup Champion. Kathy has competed for the USET at the 1989 World Cup in Gothenburg, Sweden and at the 1989 North American Championships, and has served as a member of the USET Active Riders Council. She has trained extensively in Europe with Ernst Bachinger and Herbert Rehbein. Kathy has trained many horses and riders to the FEI levels. Among her own Grand Prix horses have been Enterprise and Beethoven. After training Beethoven to Grand Prix, Kathy sold him to a German rider in 1993. Shortly thereafter, Beethoven began winning at Grand Prix in Germany.

Kathy studied at the University of Vienna, and received her BA from Simmons College in Boston. She resides and trains at her farm, Apple Valley, in Harvard, Massachusetts.

Photo on page 30.

Robert Dover

Coming out of retirement in 1992 after nearly two years, two-time Olympic veteran Robert Dover won the USET Olympic Selection Trails in Clarcona, Florida with victories in both the Grand Prix and Grand Prix Special. Earlier in the season, he captured the Grand Prix and Grand Prix Special at the CDI American Dressage Concours. Riding Lectron, he was a member of the bronze medal winning U.S. team at the Barcelona Olympics.

With Federleicht, Robert was a member of the 1988 Olympic Team. He was the highest placed American, finishing 13th individually. First long listed by the USET in 1977, Robert made his international debut as a member of the 1984 Olympic Team with Romantico. This pair were also members of the gold medal team at the North American Dressage Championships in 1985.

Robert credits much of his success to the late Col. Bengt Ljungquist, his trainer for many years. He has also trained with Herbert Rehbein of Germany. A member of the 1986 World Championship Team and a five-time National Freestyle Champion, Robert spent 1987 competing in Europe with Federleicht and Juvel. His many successes there included winning the Grand Prix Freestyle in Aachen, as well as wins in Rotterdam, Hanover and Zuidlaren. He was also leading rider at Hanover and Brussels. Robert and Federleicht completed their winter in Europe by placing fourth in the 1988 Dressage World Cup.

Robert won the 1989 Miller's/USET National Dressage Championship on Walzertakt. Robert led his teammates to the team gold medal at the 1989

North American Dressage Championship in Quebec, Canada, while also capturing the individual silver medal. He was the highest scoring member of the bronze medal winning U.S. Team at the 1994 World Equestrian Games in Holland riding Devereaux.

Photo on page 39.

Pamela Goodrich

Pam started riding ponies on the family farm before she could walk. In 1971, she graduated from Morven Park International Equestrian Institute in Virginia. After graduation, she began to go to Portugal for several months each year to train with Nuno Olivera. She also spent four years training with Michael Poulin while operating her own teaching and training facility in Meriden, Connecticut.

In 1989, Pam married Pierre St. Jacques and moved to her current home in Canada where the pair own and operate Le Club Equestre.

Photo on page 43.

Anne Gribbons

Anne was born in Stockholm, Sweden, and educated both in Sweden and the United States. She has trained with Col. Bengt Ljungquist, Harry Boldt, Herbert Rehbein, and Dr. Volker Moritz. She has schooled a number of horses to Grand Prix and brought several students to the FEI levels.

Anne was a member of the USET squad at the North American Championships in 1985, represented the U.S. at the World Championships in Canada in 1986 and was first alternate to the USET Pan American team in 1991. She has earned the USDF Bronze, Silver and Gold rider medals. Her horses have won numerous AHSA and USDF awards. Kristall was USDF Horse of the Year at First Level in 1981, at Prix St. Georges in 1984 and at Intermediare Freestyle in 1986. Metallic was AHSA Champion at First and Second Levels (1988 and 1989), both with the highest score in the nation.

Anne is an FEI C judge and a licensed AHSA I judge. During 1991-92 she chaired the Active Competitors Committee of the USET and since 1992 Anne has been a member of the AHSA Board of Directors.

Photo on page 48.

Ann Guptill

Ann is a dressage rider, trainer and instructor based in southern Connecticut, riding horses of all types and teaching riders on all levels. She also maintains an active competition schedule.

Ann and Maple Magnum first achieved national prominence at the 1987 Pan American Games, where as a member of the USET they helped the team earn a silver medal and were placed fifth individually. They were also the highest scoring Americans in the team competition. Since then, the pair has been on the USET training and long lists, rising steadily up the FEI ranks with many important wins.

Ann and her family currently own and operate Fox Ledge Farm, a dressage training facility in East Haddam, Connecticut.

Photo on page 53.

Bent Jensen

Born in Copenhagen, Denmark, Bent has been riding since the age of seven. For five years he was a student of the world renowned Olympic silver medalist Lis Hartel. Ms. Hartel is best remembered for her inspirational performances at the 1952, 1954 and 1956 Olympics while suffering partial paralysis from polio. In 1984 and again in 1985, Bent was recognized by the Danish Riding Association for achieving the highest year end scores and was awarded the title National Rider of the Year.

Bent left Denmark in 1986 to work as the head trainer at Southgate Farm in Florida. While at Southgate, he trained the Danish warmblood stallion Ariston and in 1989 he won the World Cup Qualifying Finals in Venice, Florida. He was also awarded the title Grand Prix Champion by the New England Dressage Association. In 1990 and again in 1992, Bent came in first place in the five Grand Prix classes that he entered at the Palm Beach Derby.

In 1990 and 1992, Bent competed in several internationally acclaimed shows such as Goodwood, Aachen, and Paris. In 1992, he rode as a member of the Danish Olympic team in Barcelona. He continues to compete in CDI shows in the U.S. and CDIO shows abroad.

The many horses successfully trained by Bent include Honduras, Indigenous, Discreet, Matisse, Mendelson, Timor, Grand Garcon and Royalist.

Photo on page 57.

Carol Lavell

Riding Gifted, Carol won the 1991 Miller's/USET National Grand Prix Championship. She also won the Volvo World Cup U.S. League Final in 1991 and then placed fourth at the 1992 World Cup Finals, matching the highest placing ever by a U.S. rider. She followed her World Cup performance with a Grand Prix win at CDI-Goodwood. Gifted was named 1991 Horse of the Year. In 1992, Carol and Gifted were members of the U.S. team which took the bronze medal at the Barcelona Olympics. In 1994, Carole was a member with Gifted of the U.S. Team at the World Equestrian Games in Holland, where the team captured the bronze medal.

Carol was the highest placed American rider (13th overall) at the 1990 World Dressage Championships in Stockholm, Sweden on Gifted. She and Gifted were also Reserve Champions in the 1990 Miller's/USET Dressage Championship. Her 1990 season culminated with her selection as Female Equestrian Athlete of the year by the U.S. Olympic Committee.

In 1989, Carol was double gold medalist at the North American Dressage Championship, where Gifted became the first American horse since Keen in 1979 to win an individual title at a major international event. Carol also won individual and team silver medals at the 1987 Pan American Games.

Carol, a native of Rhode Island, has brought home many national championships from First Level to Grand Prix, and has ridden several horses to Horse of the Year awards.

Photo on page 64.

Belinda Nairn

Belinda was born in Wellington, New Zealand and now resides in Coatesville, Pennsylvania. Her current dressage partner is Disney, an eight year old Dutch warmblood gelding.

Belinda was a member of the U.S. Olympic dressage team in 1988 and won the individual bronze medal at the U.S. Olympic Festival in 1989. In 1991, she won both the individual and team gold medals at the Olympic Festival.

Photo on page 76.

Carole Grant Oldford

Carole resides in Fenton, Michigan, and is not only a recognized AHSA judge and a member of the USET Planning Committee but also the mother of two daughters who are successful horsewomen. Mary Ann Northrop has followed in her mother's footsteps by competing in dressage and Tonya Grant is a successful hunter/jumper rider, trainer, and instructor.

As a successful competitor, Carole has many highlights in her career. These include the bronze medal at the Los Angeles Olympic Festival with Tolerant in 1991, the silver medal at the Texas Olympic Festival with Tolerant and sixth place at the USET Intermediare I championship with Tolerant in 1993. Carole and Tolerant were members of the USET Can-Am gold medal team, also in 1993.

Photo on page 93.

Jessica Ransehousen

Jessica rode Forstrat on the 1960 Olympic Team at the age of 22. She also rode Forstrat in the 1964 Olympics and Orpheus in the 1988 Olympics. She was on the silver medal team at the Pan American Games in 1959 and rode again on the Pan Am Team in 1963 in São Paulo, Brazil, but was unable to complete because Forstrat was injured.

Jessica was the most successful woman dressage rider at CDIO in Aachen, Germany in 1958 and was third in Zuidlaren, Holland in 1987 and fifth in the Special in Brussels, Belgium in 1987.

She is an AHSA I dressage judge and FEI I judge. She also is USET vice president for dressage and serves on the AHSA Dressage Committee and the AHSA FEI Rules Committee.

Photo on page 112.

Gary Rockwell

Gary trained with Lilian Roye in Pennsylvania and Jorge Olsen in Denmark. He is a trainer and instructor and imports Danish horses with the help of Olsen.

Gary has many AHSA and USDF awards to his credit. He was a member of the gold medal winning East team at the 1990 U.S. Olympic Festival. Gary has competed successfully abroad in Germany and Holland. In 1994, he won the Grand Prix at the CDI in Palm Beach, Florida riding the Danish mare Suna. He and Suna were also part of the bronze medal winning U.S. team at the 1994 World Equestrian Games in The Netherlands.

Photo on page 123.

Jane Savoie

Jane is from Randolph Center, Vermont. She was the 1992 USET Olympic Dressage Team's reserve rider with the eleven year old Dutch warmblood Zapatero. Jane is the author of *That Winning Feeling!*, a book that explores the science of positive mind power as it relates to riding and training. She travels extensively to lecture on mental training and to teach dressage clinics.

Photo on page 137.

CHAPTER 1

The Levels and Their Requirements

I'm just starting out in dressage and would like to show. What are the minimum requirements to show at Training Level?

Training Level is your foundation — those are your basics upon which everything is built. The five basics are: relaxation, forward movement, regular rhythm, straightness and lastly, obedience. That is your foundation. In succeeding levels you don't lose any of those qualities. You add to those qualities. Just as a house that isn't built on a strong foundation is going to fall in a storm, you are going to run into difficulties at some point if you haven't established those five things from the beginning.

Jane Savoie

I like to see three really good basic gaits that are ridden forward in a rhythm. I want to get the feeling that the horse's gaits are being maximized by the rider — that the horse is accepting the bit, moving easily from the leg, and has achieved a minimum amount of bending and balance required at Training Level.

Gary Rockwell

A horse that is willingly going forward, stays on reasonably steady contact and remains on the aids in transitions. He should not fall on the rider's leg in turns and circles. If his concentration isn't one hundred percent, and he plays a little without getting out of hand, that's no crime at this level. Obviously, the quality of his natural gaits plays a large part in evaluating the total picture.

The first requirement of all horses as they start in their training is that they learn to move forward. So I am looking to make sure that the horse has sufficiently met the requirement of moving forward from the rider's aids. Then I would look for the second requirement, and that is of straightness, so that the horse would be learning at Training Level to move straight on straight lines and bent on bent lines with the hind legs following in the footprints of the front feet on the same side so that the horse looked like the segment of the straight line and circle that he is moving along.

With those two qualities of forward motion and proper straightness, the rider, at Training Level, should start to regulate the amounts of those qualities through the use of the third requirement, the outside rein. That is the rein of opposition and it regulates the amounts of the first two. So you should see, therefore, the forward motion being regulated so that it's just the exact amount that the rider would need from the horse and that produces regularity of steps, and you should also see at the same time the maintenance of proper bend and proper straightness which would itself start the horse learning the idea of stretching towards the ground. And so those basic principles together would make the horse appear to me that he was stretching nicely forward into the bridle, having the desire to go towards the ground and round his frame and maintain regularity and rhythm and balance.

Robert Dover

The main thing is that I see harmony — that there is no fighting going on between the rider's hand and the horse's mouth which is what you see most of the time. The horse doesn't have to be truly on the bit for me. If the horse is moving into the bit, and there's no fighting and the horse is bending and going forward, I think it's okay for Training Level.

Charlotte Bredahl

Real evenness in the stride — not getting quick or slowing down too much in turns or straight ahead, nice steady bend, not too much falling on the forehand, good transitions.

Jessica Ransehousen

Basically, you want to see a horse that's accepting the aids and quietly going forward in a good rhythm. The frame is not so important as that they are happy in their job, they're accepting the aids and they're forward. Accuracy is going to win the Training Level test.

Ann Guptill

I like to see that the horse is in a natural carriage, meaning the walk, trot, and canter he does in the test should resemble the walk, trot, and canter he does free, except that he is under control of the rider and accepting of the aids. That allows a lot of difference in the frame of the horse, depending on his natural movement and balance. Horses that are built more on the forehand, like the Thoroughbred and Quarter Horse, should be more open, meaning traveling a little in front of the vertical, stepping out to the reins, so that they can keep their balance. Horses with a higher head and neck can go in a rounder frame so that they travel more through their back.

Pam Goodrich

What characteristics do you expect to see in a good Training Level horse?

We returned from Lamplight Show in August, 1993 and we did two back to backs with five German judges that nobody knew, and one of the biggest things they said which I agree with is that the nose must be in front of the vertical. And again and again they said, "The neck is too short." Of course the horses have to accept the bit but I don't want to see short necks and long rear ends in Training Level. And I'd like to have a feeling that the horses take their hind legs and fill up their withers. And I really hate when the horse's poll drops behind the ears too much. I think that's a problem you'll live with for a long time if you teach your four and five year olds that.

Carol Grant Oldford

What I like to see is a simpatico picture. Above all, a horse that is moving forward freely and accepting the bit in balance, naturally and without resistance or fear. I would like to see the horse straight, although this is a bit difficult at this level, as the horse is green, and still learning straightness. Intrinsic to the horse's balance, is that he has begun to develop an understanding of half-halts, which would be reflected in the regularity of his gaits and transitions. Obviously, a certain degree of obedience is necessary to score well at Training Level, but I don't mind some playfulness, as this is kindergarten and the horse's first exposure to shows and all. The correct training is more important than a few behavioral bloops.

Kathy Connelly

What is expected at First Level?

I'm a great believer in keeping more horses in the First Level than most people like to do. The minute they can do the figures they think they should do Second. I'm one of these people who thinks you really should start to get the horse a little more collected before you go to Second. As a judge, I see too many horses that are too strung out and trying to do the Second Level figures and I'd like to see a little bit more of the horse being able to be slightly more compressed and not so quite downhill in the front.

Jessica Ransehousen

In First and Second Level I really expect the horses to be on the bit and forward for the whole test. And again, bending. You don't see a lot of bending usually, and I like to see more of that. Especially through corners you just see the hind legs always flying out.

Charlotte Bredahl

The same as in Training Level, but with an added amount of self-carriage and a visible transition between lengthened and working gaits.

Anne Gribbons

I like to see a greater improvement in the horse's understanding and acceptance of the half-halt. Certainly this continues to apply as the horse graduates from level to level. As the horse develops greater strength and agility he is more able to accept weight on his hind end as the result of correctly ridden half-halts. At First Level, the horse is beginning to discover how to balance the range of his movement as he lengthens his trot and canter and then resumes the working gait again after the lengthening. While the horse is learning more about his hind legs for engagement, and the elements of straightness I expect to see him accept contact without restriction or tenseness — obedient but relaxed.

Kathy Connelly

How do you envision the progression from Training through Second Levels?

As you progress from Training Level you've just begun teaching the horse that it's possible for him to balance himself without the use of his head and neck being thrown upwards or excessive swishing of his tail, by being straight on straight lines, bent on bent lines and forward without speeding up which produces regularity.

Gwen Blake riding Juvel, in the extended trot. Photo courtesy of Donida Farm.

From that we use these three sets of aids that we have, the driving aid, the bending aid and the aid of the rein of opposition to begin in what you would call the marriage of those sets of aids into the half-halt.

And from First Level on, even from after you've begun Training Level on, you'd start to teach the horse what the half-halt really means to him and that it is the bringing of the horse to the perfect state of balance and attention. So through the use of the half-halts, you see the maturation of the horse from one level to the next level by his ability to accept the half-halt in a better and more effective and efficient way by bringing his hind legs better underneath him, finding that balance and then also learning at these lower levels what it is to yield away from the pressure of the rider's leg in what is the leg-yield and then from there in the higher parts of the First Level and then in Second Level into the beginning of the lateral movements or exercises like shoulder-in, haunches-in, because the haunches-in on a diagonal line is a half-pass. Even by Second Level you can be working at the beginnings of those movements. With those movements and with the increased use of half-halts, you're bringing the horse by the Second Level toward the state of collection which is his greater ability to bear weight on his hind legs and to produce the beautiful arched frame that we see as the levels become higher in dressage.

Robert Dover

What do you like to see as the horse is developing First and Second Level?

I like to see a good horizontal balance, meaning they are not quite so free. The rider has some effect now on the horse. The First and Second Level horse should be able to maintain a horizontal balance without a lot of restriction in the stride, but I don't expect it to be as free as a training level horse. They should be able to maintain the gait and balance on smaller circles and lateral movements. They should be on the aids, that means they should willingly follow the indications of the rider's legs, seat, and hands. They should also be able to show the beginning of changes of pace within the gait - lengthening and shortening of stride, and, in Second Level, to show the ability to start shifting more weight to the hind legs in beginning collection.

Pam Goodrich

I'd like to see a horse that really accepts the leg and moves away from it. By the time the horse has gotten to First Level I want to see that he will lengthen in trot and that he will come back. And if I see a wonderful horse going to the First Level and then the lengthening comes up and he can't do that, I think there's something wrong in the progression. And it doesn't have to be for a ten but it has to be within his capabilities o f good elasticity because without a correct lengthening at that level, it is difficult to develop a good medium later. Also that the horse accepts the leg in leg-yielding and doesn't just make mincing steps.

Carol Grant Oldford

I like to see increased steadiness in hand, the beginning of collection, and enough strength behind to carry himself in an even rhythm at all gaits. There should be clearer transitions between working, collected and extended gaits. As a judge, one rarely sees true collection at this level, unless the horse is an old campaigner who has been dropped down the levels.

Anne Gribbons

What more does the judge want to see at Third and Fourth Level?

In my mind it is a systematic progression and I don't skip levels. Everything builds from the level before so at Training Level we have those five qualities I mentioned. Then at First Level you begin to see the addition of suppleness, a horse's ability to smoothly change his balance forward and back such as in lengthenings and side to side such as in serpentines. From First Level on, it is a systematic development of contact and collection. As a horse becomes more collected, there is a progressive loading of the hind legs. The center of gravity is shifted towards the hind legs which results in a lightening of the forehand.

Jane Savoie

The self-carriage should be consistent, the forehand somewhat raised and the haunches lowered. Transitions ought to be well defined, balanced on the haunches and light in hand. Engagement should not fade in the counter canter, in circles or in turns. Responses to the aids should be prompter by now, and collection must be reliably "installed."

Anne Gribbons

The horse has begun to shift his weight to the hindquarters and he clearly shows a contrast between collected and medium and extended gaits. By this level, he should have achieved a degree of engagement and lightness of the forehand as well as obedience to the rider and accuracy in the test.

Gary Rockwell

Third and Fourth Level horses have to be a lot more balanced, a lot more supple and submissive. I don't mind if they are having to struggle a little bit because of the increased difficulty of the collection. The horses that are big, free movers often have difficulty at this level because they are having to learn to shorten the stride and carry more weight behind. They often will look constrained until they are strong enough to carry the new balance with ease. I like to see more carriage and freedom. However, many of the really good horses lose a little bit at these levels and gain it back at Prix St. Georges, because they are not strong enough to be able to keep their balance in the collection and keep their big movement. It's a bad stage, and as a horse trainer I understand that they go through it in trying to learn collection. They can't do it like an FEI horse, so they have to do it however they can in the beginning.

Pam Goodrich

At Third Level you have to see the horse making real definitions. You've got to see more activity, you've got to see more of a frame, the horse being a little higher in the poll and a little bit more engaged behind. Those are the things that I think are missing the most. A lot of people don't spend quite enough time on the basics and they get running around doing the figures and not really thinking about whether they're correct.

Jessica Rausehousen

At Third and Fourth Level you just need to see more engagement.

Charlotte Bredahl

Obviously, the greater degree of collection. By Third and Fourth Level the rider has to be very accurate. The whole test must present a nice picture with flow between the movements. Transitions have to be accurate but not abrupt. The horse must be able to carry himself in the same balance in all three gaits, which is difficult at these levels because often the horse is learning flying changes at Third Level, may not be confirmed in them, and may have a little bit of difficulty in it. The test that's going to win at Third and Fourth Level is a horse who can execute all of the movements and give a smooth appearance to the test and be able to carry himself in the same balance throughout the test.

Ann Guptill

I think the horse must become beautiful at Third and Fourth Level. Even a horse that started as an unattractive sort, by Third and Fourth Level should have developed a topline and have developed its gaits. The balance should be such that the horse is achieving more engagement and more lightness of the forehand which allows him to perform the required movements.

Gary Rockwell

I think his strength is now getting better so he can show better transitions. He can show medium canters that lengthen, and he can come back and sit down. He mustn't at Third or Fourth run around the corners anymore, and quality and strength should be improving. I like to see a horse with big steps. Even a small horse can have big, beautiful gaits.

Carol Grant Oldford

As a judge, what are some of the common problems you see at Third and Fourth Levels?

I see a lot of people who go on before they should go on. I see a lot of horses at Second or Third level that really should do a Training Level, because the horses

Charlotte Bredahl riding Monsieur at the extended trot. (Photo courtesy of Charlotte Bredahl)

are really not truly on the bit, and they're not really bending, and a lot of them are not really going forward. Trying to do the movement is only hurting the horses and the riders too for that matter, because the basics are not there. And a lot of times I'll recommend to people that they go back. Of course they don't want to hear that, but I do it anyway. At Fourth Level a lot of times you see horses pulled together in front rather than true engagement.

Charlotte Bredahl

The base behind too wide which is hard to see in a very talented horse, but which shows up again later in piaffe and passage. At Third and Fourth I'd still like to see relaxation at the walk, I mean there are special horses like Rembrandt who think like that and there are also horses like Lectron, who can walk for a ten.

Carol Grant Oldford

Gaps in training, reflected by incorrectness in collection, and subsequently in the medium and extended gaits. A common problem is a horse that lacks proper engagement and suppleness and therefore is too short in his neck and unhappy in the bridle. Training Level through Fourth Level are our national levels. The goal is to produce a horse in an organized evolutionary training process to complete these levels and commence the FEI levels if he has that level of talent to continue on. A common problem is that horses lose quality in their gaits and in their basics, as riders strive to train and show the more difficult movements at these levels. The rider must maintain perspective to know when the horse's physical strength and training and his understanding and confidence level are synchronized. Some riders accelerate a horse's training program at the wrong stage for the horse in order to make a certain show schedule, and find out the hard way that it does not work. Every stride we ride is training. It's either correct training or incorrect training. Any area that is skipped or skimmed over will catch up with us. It is better to stay a level lower until the horse catches up with himself. So the common problems show in the horse's ability to maintain forwardness as he learns collection. Oftentimes, we see the increased power and activity of the hind legs hampered rather than harnessed and directed.

Kathy Connelly

CHAPTER 2

Contact and Half-Halts

The concept of contact is hard to teach and hard to learn. What is your conception of the correct contact?

Proper contact was described to me by Colonel Bengt Ljungquist, and I have never found a way to put it better. This is what he said: "If you take a piece of flat bark from a tree, close your fingers around it and put it in a running stream of water, you will feel a gentle and steady tug on your hand. That is the feel you should strive to have when you ride: a live but comfortable connection with the horse's mouth and the sensation that he wants to take you forward while staying in constant communication."

Anne Gribbons

Basically, when a horse is on the bit, he goes forward into your hand so you better have a contact that is inviting before you even attempt to ride a half-halt. It is unfair to say to the horse, 'step into my hand' if the hand is not a good hand. And so I spend a bit of time explaining contact. The qualities that I cover are that the contact should be firm, consistent, elastic, with one bearing on the rein. The degree of firmness depends on the degree of self-carriage. With a Training Level horse, I would say a solid one or two pounds. A horse will accept a contact that is even too firm as long as the arms are elastic. This is preferable to a contact that is too light and jabs him in the mouth with every step he takes. Consistent means that the straight line from bit to hand to elbow never changes. The contact does not go slack and then tight. Elastic. When you think of elastic, think of your elbows. In the walk and the canter your elbow joints have to open and close in a forward and backward motion to allow for the movement of the horse's head and neck. In rising trot the head and neck of the horse are steady but the rider goes up and down so the elbows must open and close in an up and down motion. The elasticity of the elbows allows for movement, whether it's the movement of the horse's head and neck or the movement of the rider. The idea of bearing on the rein is that you give to the horse the feeling in his mouth that the reins are in one hand. I often have riders put the reins in one hand and then put the reins back in the two hands and make it feel that it is the same. People say "my horse is uneven in the rein" but if you're not offering a contact that is absolutely even, how can you expect the horse to be even in the rein? Your hands should be symmetrical and the mirror-image of each other in order to give the feeling that the reins are in one hand.

Jane Savoie

What part does forwardness play in training a horse to accept contact?

First in the training of the horse, utmost, always and imperatively comes forwardness. We must teach our horses to move willingly and spontaneously from a "light" leg. A forward-thinking horse reflects desire and enthusiasm. Forwardness is a state of mind, not just a physical trait ridden into the horse. Only then will it be consistently produced by the horse in all gaits and movements in training and in the competitive arena.

Kathy Connelly

I really want to stress with all the riders that are training and learning, I'm sure they pretty much know that the basic number one priority is to keep the horse moving forward and I think sometimes that's a lost concept. I just want to make sure that they know that will follow them clear through Grand Prix. I think that really needs to be stressed to all the young riders who are coming up. The basics are what need to be kept up with. The movements will become less difficult.

Gwen Blake

I've heard many ways of describing the half-halt. What is a half-halt?

The half-halt is the bringing of the horse to a perfect state of balance and attention — that is it by definition. What we do to make a half-halt occur is to marry the three sets of aids that we have in dressage riding which are the basic principles that we go by. Those sets of basics are the driving aids: The two legs and the seat; the bending aids which produce straightness, which are the two legs — inner leg at the girth, outer leg behind the girth, and the inner rein which brings the head and neck in with the bend created in the horse's body from your legs; and the rein of opposition, the outside rein. By closing the outside hand into a fist we close an imaginary door in front of the horse's face which if open would allow him to speed up as we use our driving and bending aids, but if closed, says to him, no, you have to stay here for a second. Because he yields to that action of the outer rein being closed into a fist, and at the same time understands that he is being driven, he comes underneath himself with his hind legs more, bending the joints of his hind legs. At that second, as he lowers his croup because he has bent his hind legs more, the front end raises up, but since he's yielded from the action of the outer hand, it comes up from the withers and it produces that beautiful arch that we have in dressage.

Robert Dover

My definition of a half-halt is an aid to rebalance a horse, by activating the hind legs. Through the levels of training, of course, the result changes as a horse advances. In the beginning I like to teach the horse and rider to develop the half-halt by slowly developing the strength of the horse through transitions. Specifically one I like to use is the trot-walk transition. I start by doing maybe five or six walk steps and back to the trot and then again five or six walk steps and back to the trot. It's important that the horse stay balanced through the downward transition and keeps a clear walk into the transition back up to the trot. As this is obtained, I try to shorten the number of steps and work towards one step of walk. Then it seems that the rider has the correct aids to close and drive under the horse's hind legs without stopping the forward motion.

Gwen Blake

I think I understand the concept of half-halt, but how do I ride one correctly?

How to go about doing it? The half-halt has to be ridden with the thought of the seat and the legs being used a fraction of a second earlier than the closing of the hand because otherwise you get what I call, 'too much halt and not enough half.' You get the horse being stopped and being ridden from the front end backwards. So, as we're going, for instance on a circle to the left, the rider would have inner leg at the girth, outer leg behind the girth, the inside rein would be doing its usual job of being closed just enough to produce the bend of the head and neck equal to that which you've achieved in the horse's body from your legs, and at the second when you would produce the half-halt, the rider would then tighten the seat, tighten the back and produce what is called a braced back and then drive with the seat as if the

Kathy Connelly and Beethoven in passage. Photo by Tony De Costa.

rider was driving the cantle of the saddle towards the pommel of the saddle or a swing forward. At that second the closing of the legs and that driving seat makes the horse have the desire to increase both in speed and in bend, because the inner leg has been used on the girth and the outer leg has been used behind the girth. At that same second we close that imaginary door in front of the horse by closing the outer hand in a fist thereby saying to him, no, you may not speed up just because I'm driving, and no, you may not bend at too great a degree just because I'm using the bending aid. The horse who has learned what that means will yield to the outside hand and will maintain his rhythm, the same rhythm that he had before the half-halt and the same rhythm that he has to go out after the half-halt, bending those joints as I just described, bringing more weight to his hindquarters, a more supple, beautiful and mobile front end and then with that the rider has reward his having done this by once again opening the closed outside hand and relaxing that tightened driving seat. And at that second we open the door back saying, okay horse, now you can proceed forward but now with a new state of balance and attention. The only thing is that the half-halt is a matter of degrees and so even though I described the use of the seat, the legs and the rein, the half-halt in an upward transition will be relatively different than the half-halt in a downward transition. The upward transition would be normally with a driving seat, the closing of the lower leg through the closing of the outer hand. Since we don't want to have the horse drop his back, the downward transition is more reliable when we use a braced back, but don't drive with it. It's what we call a stilled seat. And then the closing of the leg, again, but now more of the closing of the upper leg, by using the upper leg more instead of the lower leg, you slightly lighten the seat which has been braced, and you ask the horse to come up with his back up to the rider's seat and then you use the least amount of outer hand necessary to produce the downward transition in harmony.

Robert Dover

The important thing for the rider is to make sure he uses his back and leg, not just his hand. What I try to do if they are on a horse that has a really good trot is instead of asking for half-halts, if the horse is in a good horizontal position — which I try to get however I can — is to ask them to make transitions within the trot without using their hands, keeping the same hands, just so that they learn to adjust the trot with their backs. When they can do that, they can start to learn how to do transitions that actually shift weight to the rear without paralyzing the body of the horse. And again so much depends on the horse. If you're on a big tanky horse that likes to power-off the hind legs, doing halts helps to shift weight back to the hindquarters. When the horse dives on his nose, say no, that was done on the front legs. And having the rider feel the difference in all the transitions until they get one where the horse shifts his weight to the hind legs and then ask him to go forward, then asking them to slow the trot down but get the same feeling that they had when they did the halt.

Horses that are more sensitive and not tanky that way just need little reminders. I do transitions in shoulder-in. Do shoulder-in, then slow the trot down, then go back to a more forward trot and back to a slower trot until the rider feels that the horse shifts weight back in the shorter trot in shoulder-in and when asked to go forward, the horse has a bigger, more uphill trot. Then the rider can attempt to do the same thing straight ahead.

Pam Goodrich

Basically you close your legs, and get the feeling of asking for a lengthening but rather than letting the horse express that energy over the ground, you contain that energy within his body by closing the outer hand in a fist for three seconds. Now, the only problem with that is three seconds is a long time and if you close your outside hand for three seconds the horse is going to bend his neck to the outside and therefore, he is not straight. One of the rules of half-halts is that in order for them to work, the horse must be forward and the horse must be straight. So to the degree that you need it, apply soft squeezes on the inner hand (bending aids) to maintain the straightness. I use the inner rein very judiciously because riders find that if they move the bit in the horse's mouth, the horse will flex in the jaw. This can be dangerous because if you flex the jaw without getting the horse over the back first, then the horse feels lovely in your hand but you don't know that you don't have him connected. So the squeezes on the inner rein are not to get the horse to give in the jaw, the squeezes on the inner rein are to counter the action of the closed outside hand so that the body of the horse stays straight. Even though these aids are put on almost simultaneously, freeze-frame photography would show the legs close first, then the outside hand close in a fist, then, if needed, the vibrating inner rein.

Jane Savoie

It seems that half-halt doesn't mean the same thing to everyone.

To me, there are two different types of half-halts. One is used for steadying the horse and the other is used for more activation. When you think of a half-halt, you want to think about whether you're making just a steadying pressure — i.e., the horse who is getting a little bit too forward in movement and not quite staying under your seat. That kind of a half-halt would be a steadying half-halt which takes maybe a stride or two. You draw back in front and you close your legs a little bit. You hold your upper body and elbows a little bit back and the horse stays a little back and is steady. And you keep trying. The other is like when you make a hesitation half-halt where you make the horse actually hesitate a little bit in the trot. This is probably over two strides in the trot, and you draw the horse back and you activate him quite nicely with the leg or the stick. First of all make him hesitate a little and then you make him engage a little bit more and then you go on.

Jessica Ransehousen

I know that I can ride an effective half-halt but I'm at a loss as to how to explain and teach it to my students.

I find it difficult to teach riders if they've had some incorrect training. They tend to just want to pull on one rein or stop the horse completely and that's not what it is. They have to learn to rebalance the horse. I often teach the half-halt without really saying "this is the half-halt." I start a lot of them out on circles where they can maintain the bend which therefore is easier for them to keep the frame and the balance. When this is achieved, I send them off to the straight line.

Gwen Blake

I go back to the lateral work. We also use a lot of turns on the forehand, because even though it's a very basic movement, it makes the horse connect from the hind legs to the hand. That's where the lack of understanding is with a lot of riders is how to get the feel from the hind leg to the hand. The turns on the forehand help, because the rider has to apply the rein and the leg on the same side and have the hind leg on the same side step up into that rein. They can feel the different effect their aids have on each side of the horse and how the two sides of their horse are different and that will help them understand the straightness, too. Because it's done at a walk, it slows the whole process down. They can feel step by step the horse's response. When a rider understands the connection of hand to hind leg and leg into hand they will be able to make a more effective half halt.

Ann Guptill

I tell my students that you're doing one of two things when you're riding: ideally, following the horse's mouth or meeting him with your hand. If you put your leg on the horse, that indicates 'go' or 'activate.' If you want the horse to go forward, you put your leg on and you allow the hand; if you want the horse to come together, you put your leg on as if you want to go forward and as he goes forward, you only allow to come through the rein what it is that you want, which is bringing him more together. It is necessary for the rider to have achieved a position on the horse and an ability to coordinate his aids. I usually start working on a serpentine, asking for a few shorter, more active steps each time we cross the centerline. With that vague idea, we begin a long process of attempts and connections which, over a long period of time produces the concept of the half-halt. The difficulty comes with coordinating the rider's entire body and in developing a "feel" for what the horse is doing, i.e., when to release after the half-halt is accomplished. The timing comes with more and more riding.

Gary Rockwell

The effect of the half-halt is determined by so many things. I try to always start teaching people through a little shoulder-in so that they don't block the hind legs. I have them do simple transitions, trot-walk-trot, always in a little bit of shoulder-in so that the aid is not backwards but forwards and the hind leg doesn't step back or stop. It's asked to continue to step so that when they apply the downward transition or the shortening aid, it affects the hind leg but doesn't stop it. This is the biggest problem 99% of people have in the half-halts: they stop the power of the hind leg rather than harnessing it.

Pam Goodrich

I think the only way to teach it, especially in the beginning, is just by making people do transitions. I think that's the only way they can grasp it. I always make my riders do lots of just trot-walk transitions which basically means practicing their half-halts, and closing their legs and supporting the horse on the outside rein. I work a lot on getting people to bring the horses from the inside leg to the outside rein. You see a lot of people always hanging on the inside rein. I do a lot of work to correct that. A lot of times I have people do a transition, for example, from trot to walk or walk to trot I have them leg yield a couple of steps in the transition. And the same when they go back — they leg yield a couple of steps and then they walk and then the horses don't get totally disconnected in the transition.

Charlotte Bredahl

As a rider, I find it easier to teach a horse to do a half-halt than it is as an instructor to teach a person how to ride a half-halt. It is difficult for students, sometimes, to learn the coordination and application of the aids. It seems so abstract and esoteric, in the beginning, to learn what a half-halt is. The two main questions that most students ask are; one: How often do you repeat the half-halt, and two: How long and how strong should the half-halt be. These two questions are answered through experience. The experience comes through riding different horses over a period of time. What counts here is the rider's ability to understand and conceptualize what the horse's response was from the previous half-halts. That is a matter of feel. Instructors can teach theory and they can teach exercises, but they cannot teach feel. Riders learn it with practice and experience.

So, the method that I use to teach half-halts to riders is a four step process.

Part 1: The combined use of the seat and leg to bring the horse forward to the bit, straight into the reins. Part 2: The rider closes both hands softly (more use of the outside rein because the rider is riding with the inside leg to the outside rein, the collecting rein) until the horse comes through and responds softly in the reins. Part

3: The rider softens in response to the horse's softening. Part 4: The rider rides the horse forward again to maintain activity in the hind legs and not to block them. Of course, this happens in a matter of a second or seconds. It is important to have the horse light to the leg so that he makes an active response with his hind legs, willingly forward and through to the bridle. The rider must have proper contact and a rewarding hand. A horse's mouth is as sensitive as our mouth is. The joints in the rider's wrist and fingers directly influence the joint of the snaffle which directly influences the horse's poll. Horses' polls are designed by nature to flex down — inward and outward longitudinally, and to bend laterally left and right. It is important that the rider maintain a relaxed and pliable wrist and fingers to influence the horse's poll in the desired way. If you make the bit a nice place to be, the horse will keep wanting to step up to it.

To practice this half-halt sequence, I instruct riders to bring the horse on a 20 meter circle in order to maintain the proper bend as the half-halts are ridden. I ask them to ride in the trot and to ride the following transition: Trot - walk a step - trot, applying the four step process described above. We repeat this exercise, until they feel that they have the hang of it. Then we do the same with canter-trot-canter transitions.

Half-halts properly ridden teach a horse about his hind legs, by activating them. Half-halts are the foundation tool in dressage.

Kathy Connelly

After first spending some time explaining forward, than some time explaining contact, I feel I've laid a foundation for half-halt which is the key to training. It just amazes me — people trying to train horses without a half-halt. It's the tool that you use to bring your horse to a more perfect state of balance. Balance is a primary issue, because horses are not made to be ridden, and they're constantly losing their balance. And it doesn't matter if it's a Training Level horse or a Grand Prix horse. When a horse is asked to do a transition for example, there is a potential loss of balance and you must have a way, the half-halt, to restore that lost balance. Simply put the half-halt is a combination of your driving aids plus your bending aids plus a rein of opposition sustained for a period of about three seconds.

Jane Savoie

Half-halts can be described until the instructor turns blue in the face, but never truly understood by the student until he has felt one. Therefore, I prefer to teach this concept on a horse that is sufficiently schooled to respond correctly if the student applies the proper aids. With the help of such a 'professor' I'll go through the routine of telling the student the reason we use half-halts: to communicate with the horse, as if picking up the phone and saying: "Hello, are you listening?" before giving him an aid, to help him balance, slow down or collect and to increase his engagement. After explaining why, I try to tell the student how to momentarily close his legs, push down and forward with his seatbones and close his hands around the reins at the same time. Next I ask him to put it into practice by trotting the horse forward and then asking him to make 'half of a halt' without permitting the horse to come to a stop and to immediately ride forward when he feels the horse responding. Eventually the student hits on just the right amount of driving and restraining aids. After that, we can talk about half-halts and be speaking the same language. To teach half-halts to a novice rider on a green horse tends to produce confusion for both horse and rider and not a small amount of frustration for all involved.

Anne Gribbons

CHAPTER 3

Engagement and Self-Carriage

Q

What does *Durchlassigkeit* mean? And how do I get it?

Durchlassigkeit refers to the uninterrupted flow of energy from the hind end forward, and returning from the front to the hind end. It is an elastic coordination between the quarters and the forehand. *Durchlassigkeit* is the essence of elastic ballet movement in the horse. It is the essence of the horse being engaged, being forward, being straight in the reins, being light to the leg, light in the bridle. It is an essential goal in everyday practice. It requires the willingness of the horse to achieve *Durchlassigkeit*. Without it, there is no ballet.

Kathy Connelly

Durchlassigkeit (I wish we could find an English word for this!) is best promoted by half-halts which really go through and good solid transitions, especially from trot to canter and vice versa. It is maintained by keeping a consistent connection between the horse's mouth and the rider's hand at all times, thus keeping the energy that is generated from the rider's leg and seat flowing from the hocks through the back and mouth of the horse in an uninterrupted circle-like fashion. This sounds easy but is very difficult to achieve.

Anne Gribbons

Q

My horse is stiff. How do I warm him up to supple him and achieve *Durchlassigkeit*?

I think that it's very important that the horse start his warm-up stretching out and down to find the bit. During his workout, he must be willing to move from the rider's leg to a hand that allows the neck and strides to lengthen or to a hand that meets and collects him. Maintaining that willingness as you go through the levels is probably the most important aspect in achieving *Durchlassigkeit*. It's very often lost because of a rider's inability to coordinate his aids properly.

If I feel that a horse is not really lengthening and shortening his frame and stride as I want him to, I have to go backwards for awhile and retrieve it. If you don't do that, your horse may learn to make all the movements, but it might be in the end that someone will say that you don't have a very good horse, and that might not have been the case.

Gary Rockwell

I determine my plan for the day according to what my horses are able to achieve in terms of their age, their level of experience, their ability to bend, to engage, and to maintain the engagement. Often I warm up on a 20 meter circle — not too small because it is important for them to be able to use themselves freely. I usually walk them out on the trail for 15-20 minutes before any work. On the circle I make lots of transitions trot-canter-trot, until my horse feels relaxed in his back and elastic. The horse's ability in the gaits and in the transitions is indicative of what he is going to be able to do in the movements, so there is no point in proceeding to movements if the horse is not sufficiently elastic in the gaits and transitions. This is where I think we must be very careful and truthful as riders.

On the circle, I ride half-circles and passades in the trot work, because they are helpful in suppling the horse laterally and longitudinally, while maintaining a regular rhythm. Through transitions, the half-circles and passades, as the horse is able to perform these, the rider can encourage with proper half-halts, relaxation in the horses back, poll and jaw — the three obvious points of stiffness.

I also ride lengthening of stride in trot and canter, on the 20 meter circle in shoulder fore. I will lengthen for six, eight or ten strides on the circle, then collect my horse, and make an eight or ten meter circle, then lengthen again on the 20 meter circle, so that my horse learns that he can bear his weight on his hind end, and simultaneously maintain the roundness. It's important when you ride a half-halt that he does not hollow in his hack and come higher in his poll, because then his hind legs are coming out behind him and generally they are slowing too. It's important that as you ride these exercises, you ride the elastic band effect, so that the horse willingly lengthens and then collects, lengthens and then collects again, without coming behind the leg, or running through the bridle. For example, a horse that has a naturally very suspended trot, will sometimes try to make some passage as a resistance, instead of coming through. This horse must be ridden forward immedi-

Robert Dover and Lectron in passage. Photo courtesy of the USET.

ately to keep his hind legs activated and his back relaxed. The rider must be able to feel in his lower back and seat the speed of the horse's hind legs, and the feel of the horse's back so that appropriate half-halts are ridden for correction. Needless to say, this takes lots of practice. When you have achieved *Durchlassigkeit* the horse will willingly go forward light to the leg, be straight and respond well to your half-halts.

Kathy Connelly

A lot of judges have told me that my horse is behind the bit or that his poll is too low. From where I am, it looks like he is in a nice frame. What's the problem?

The horse whose poll is too low and is not moving properly forward into the hand has not met the first requirement sufficiently. If you always remember that the horse's frame is dependent upon half-halts only insofar as he has to have first accepted the basic principles of forward motion, of straightness, and marry those sets of aids into the half-halt. So I would say to the rider whose horse was behind the action of the aids and therefore too low in the frame and behind the rein, that first they have to go back and be able to receive the horse into the hand correctly by retraining the horse to the forward driving aids and with that the horse should be able to go back up to the hand successfully. And then from there you ride half-halts again, driving with the seat and leg to the hand, always when the horse arrives at the hand accepting him there and always thinking with that kind of horse that the half-halt should be as if you were asking for the medium of the gait that you are in, and only when the horse desires to go even more forward than that do you close the hand and say no faster than this. Don't think from the front end backwards. Don't think of reduction or what I call subtraction. Think of addition.

Robert Dover

Being on the bit is determined by the desire of the hind legs to step to the reins regardless of where the head and neck are, meaning with many Thoroughbred-type horses the head and neck will be up and out so they don't break in the mouth, and with many warmblood type horses they travel with a round neck, and lower poll and head behind the vertical (deep) which puts the horse through his back allowing the hindlegs to step freely forward.

. Behind the bit is when the horse is avoiding stepping with the hind legs to the reins and ducks his chin whenever the rider uses the reins or when he won't touch the reins at all.

The way you can tell as a rider which one you have is when you take on the rein gently or use the rein directly, if they're behind the rein, the chin will come further in and the horse will keep on going. If you take on the reins directly, and the horse's hind leg is stepping up to the rein, the hind leg will be affected, meaning it will step with a shorter step. If you take on the rein and the hind leg is pushing too powerfully, the horse will pull up against it. When the horse is on the bit, the reins can be used to indicate direction and lateral movements and the horse responds. When the horse is behind the bit the reins are not connected to the front end of the horse, making it difficult to turn or do lateral work.

Another indication is by the horse's response to the leg. If the horse is on the bit, application of the leg is readily accepted by the horse. For example, if the rider applies the leg to ask for a leg yield, the horse will respond. If the horse is behind the bit, and the rider applies the leg for a leg yield, the horse will not respond, or will run sideways away from the leg, because the hind leg of the horse is not stepping to the reins, consequently it is going to evade by running out to the side.

Pam Goodrich

How do you fix it when the horse comes behind the bit?

The answer is leg and a giving hand, and the problem stems from the opposite. With many riders who don't have instruction, riding the horse behind the vertical makes him more comfortable and maybe they feel he is light on the aids. But it's not correct in that it puts the horse off the aids and more on the forehand. Then what often happens is that the rider begins to enjoy sitting into his back and pushing him around. Pretty soon the back also becomes low so you have that horrible low in the stomach and low in the poll position which is a dead-end.

Gary Rockwell

Again it's a sensory feel for the riders, because riders can only see from the front of their saddle forward. They can't see what's going on behind them or to the side of them, so they tend to concentrate on what they see in front of them. Also, it takes time to develop feel through your back, seat, and legs. For a lot of lower level riders, all of their feel is through their hands and their arms. That's where lunging helps along with video taping and the use of the mirrors so that the riders can let go of that association with the front end and learn, first of all to be able to see the whole horse, and then be able to feel the whole horse.

Very often horses will give too much at the poll and come behind the vertical. This softens what the riders feel in their hands. They may have the misconception that because the horse is soft and light, that they're off their forehand. But you can look at the horse and see that the horse is behind the vertical, not taking the contact, not taking the rider forward or the rider can't perform a movement because the horse is behind the bit.

Ann Guptill

What is the difference between "behind the bit" and "poll too low"?

There are times when having the poll too low and the nose behind the vertical is not only acceptable but also desirable. The position is called "deep." It's a good stretching over the back exercise for the horse and a good warm-up frame. It's also a good position to put a horse in if he has been having difficulty learning a movement and staying over his back. If you put him a little deep, you have a better chance of keeping him connected. This position is deceivingly similar to that of a horse that is behind the bit, because in both cases the poll is low and the nose is behind the vertical. But there are some major differences that you can check to make sure you are not getting into trouble. Number one is that when a horse is deep you still have a contact. You can still feel the horse's hind legs in your hands. The horse has not dropped your hand with resulting loops in the reins. Another way to tell is the length of the horse's neck. If the poll is too low, the nose is behind the vertical, and the neck is very short with perhaps a break at the third vertebra, then you have a horse that is behind the bit. Whereas if you are riding a horse deep and the poll is too low and the nose is behind the vertical, but the neck is long, you're probably in safe territory. One is very desirable and the other is very incorrect.

Jane Savoie

This does not necessarily mean that the horse is behind the aids. Even the most confused judge can tell when a horse dips behind the vertical, but the secret lies in the other end. If the horse remains active behind and continues to follow the rider's directions without losing his forward tendency, a few steps behind the vertical does not ruin the day. Even if the judge cannot tell, it will be crystal clear to the rider when the horse is actually behind the bit, because nothing happens when he uses his driving aids. In fact, it almost feels as if the horse travels in reverse. It can be compared to driving a car when the motor suddenly shuts off and you lose both the power and the steering. It's extremely frustrating, but surely not hard to recognize.

Anne Gribbons

My trainer keeps telling me I should strive for self-carriage, but I'm not sure exactly what she means nor how to get it.

Self-carriage is one of the true reasons and rewards for all the work we put into training the horse according to classical principles, and it is easily recognizable as soon as it disappears. When your arms feel as though they are being pulled out of their sockets, when you have to kick and pull and your horse acts as though his

Pam Goodrich riding Master of the Game in the extended trot. Photo by Terri Miller.

transmission needs repair, self-carriage is the missing ingredient. A horse in good self-carriage is carrying not only himself but also the rider with the greatest of ease. He feels balanced underneath you, light but steady in your hands and he stays in front of the aids without needing constant manipulation from hands or seat. Once you have enjoyed riding a horse that carries itself, it is hard to settle for anything else.

Anne Gribbons

First of all, it has to come from the rider. They have to be able to see the whole horse. Riders who concentrate on what they see in front of them tend to ride the horses too far down and their positions tend to be down. Their heads are down, their eyes are down, their shoulders roll forward. The rider has to be in self-carriage before they can help the horse be in self-carriage. A horse in self-carriage can perform the movements of their particular level with ease and balance.

Ann Guptill

There's an ease, there's a lightness, there's a harmony that all results from that loading of the hind legs.

Jane Savoie

Self-carriage is the reward to horse and rider for a mutually understood system of harmonious aids resulting in a shared balance of two bodies as one. Because of a combination of impulsion, suppleness and the horse's ability to carry his weight on his hind end and lighten his forehand, the horse's transitions feel like a snowflake landing. The horse is able to negotiate himself laterally and longitudinally with ease at the rider's bidding. When a horse is in self carriage we have achieved *schwung*. *Schwung* is when the horse is expressing the energy and power from the hindquarters through a swinging rounded back. The horse is "through."

Kathy Connelly

CHAPTER 4

Straightness

Q I'm an event rider who always hated dressage. I always thought straightness meant that the horse went straight down the long sides. Now I realize that dressage riders have some esoteric definition of straightness. What does straightness mean in dressage?

For me it means that a horse's body parts are arranged in a straight line, symmetrically from nose to tail. His left shoulder isn't ahead of his right or the left shoulder isn't to the left and the right shoulder back and his hips to the right and things like that. Straightness is next to impossible to find, of course, because horses are either crooked because they're born that way or they're made that way by riders, which is very common. So for me straightening a horse is a continuous process of training.

There are two kinds of straightness. A horse can be straight, because he's in a straight line, and he's really straight — hind legs directly behind the shoulders traveling on a single track — that is really straight. That's reserved for God and, hopefully, Grand Prix horses who are the best in the world. Keeping Gifted straight is really difficult, because his back is a few miles long. And when he remembers that he has hind legs, they're usually not in the correct place, because the hind legs can go to the right, they can go to the left and they can go back. And whenever they go in those directions, I lose self-carriage. I want them up underneath the horse's abdomen with the hind legs directly behind the shoulders and the nose straight ahead in front, the neck coming out straight between the shoulder blades. It's not possible but it would be wonderful. I never ride my horse quite as straight as that, because I restrict development of throughness if the horse is not ready for that degree of straightness.

The second kind of straightness is straight for the work I'm requiring from the horse, not straight in the direction I'm moving. A perfect example of that is shoulder-in where you're bent around the inside leg with the shoulders placed ahead of the inside hind leg and so you are bent on a straight line. You're bent left but you're going straight ahead. So you're straight for what you're doing but not straight in the direction of the movement at all. Those are the two kinds of straightness, and both of them are extremely difficult to achieve.

Carol Lavell

Straightness means that the horse doesn't avoid going forward by swinging his haunches left or right and that he tracks straight from back to front. Almost all horses "come" more crooked to one side than the other, and it is up to the rider to make him more ambidextrous. Straightness should be strived for from the very beginning of a horse's working life. In the first year or so, it is encouraged by simply riding the horse ambitiously forward and keeping him between and in front of the legs. Later, it is enhanced and confirmed through all the bending exercises such as shoulder-in, travers, renvers and half-pass repeated constantly until the horse's suppleness and strength builds, and he can remain straight without constant reminders from the rider's aids. This problem follows the horse up the levels and cannot really be measured according to the stage of training. In short: the horse has to be made straight, the sooner, the better. As an aside, I have noticed that when a horse is laid up for a long time, not only does he lose his strength, but when you start him back into work, he tends to be as crooked as he ever was.

Anne Gribbons

Straightness is just an ongoing progression from day one. It's what horses are asked to do before they do anything else. I don't have specific exercises for teaching straightness, but I'm aware of it with each step the horse takes, and I work on making my students aware of it. You have four sides in every arena to correct for straightness.

Gary Rockwell

Straightness is essential to the whole concept of training a horse, and it is very important for riders to understand straightness and ride it correctly from the beginning because it is difficult. You want your horse's spine to be parallel to the track on which he is traveling. Horses by nature are not straight and they are not ambidextrous. The horse is broader in his hips than he is in his shoulders, therefore he will generally tend to carry his haunches to the inside of the track and his shoulders to the outside of the track. So it is up to the rider with his bending and driving aids to place the horse's shoulders slightly to the inside of the track, and the haunches onto the track. By doing this, the horse will bear his weight on his inside hind leg as he steps to the center of his body toward his outside rein. A good exercise to practice is riding down the long side or on a 20-meter circle alternating renvers and shoulder-in.

Straightness isencouraged by riding shoulder-fore. It is essential to attempt to ride the horse this way in all three gaits from a young age. Naturally, the rider must be sitting straight and centered himself to achieve this. This must be practiced, because very few people are ambidextrous by nature.

If a horse is heavy on the inside rein, it is not so much a resistance, but rather a signal, that he is crooked and his shoulders are out. It is a war of attrition to pull on the inside rein, as the heaviness is only a symptom, not the problem. So, straighten him.

To straighten a crooked horse, ride through the corner, and as soon as you are through the corner look back at the horse's inside hip. Are his hips straight with his shoulders, or are his hips in? If his hip is to the inside of the track then, with your inside leg, direct his inside hind leg to your outside rein, with your outside leg and outside supporting rein direct his shoulders to the inside leg and maintain the bend with your inside rein. (Do not cross your outside rein over the withers.) Be sure you stay centered in the saddle. When the horse is straight, he is light on the inside rein, reliably connected on the outside rein, and can be kept straight with the rider's seat and lower back. Eventually, it becomes easier, but the rider must be ever vigilant.

Kathy Connelly

There are three kinds of straight. The first is when the legs travel straight. That is when the horse comes straight toward you. You only see the front legs. The second is when the axis or spinal column of the horse is straight. That means that the horse is straight nose to tail. The third is when the energy of the horse goes in a straight line.

When the horse travels with his haunches not in line with the shoulders, for example, the shoulders are left and the haunches are right, the rider does exercises like right shoulder-in and left haunches-in. This gets the body parts under control so that they can be aligned straight. Once their legs travel straight, the rider should try and ride the axis straight. To tell if it is not straight, the rider can look down at the neck. Often he'll see an S curve in the neck, or a tilt of the head. This is due to unequal use of the hind legs or lateral stiffness. This is usually cured by bending exercises which engage, supple, and strengthen the horse. When the horse is capable of doing the lateral work evenly on both sides, they usually can travel straight with

Anne Gribbons at the shoulder-in on Leonardo II. Photo by Terri Miller.

their axis.

These two are prerequisites for the horse's energy to travel straight. When the horse is pointed in a direction and is straight in his body, he will tend to drift in one direction or another, caused by one hind leg pushing stronger than the other. This usually shows up in the more difficult movements: one tempi changes, extended trot, passage. In schooling, the rider should encourage the horse to drift in the opposite direction.

Pam Goodrich

The definition I would give is that the spine of the horse is parallel to whatever line the horse is on. So if he is on a curved line, he bends and his spine conforms to that curved line, and if he is on a straight line, his spine is straight. That is the simplest definition. Horses are like people — they are one-sided and horses tend to not want to be straight. Frequently, the problems arise from riders making the horse crooked. For instance, sometimes when riders are on a circle or a curve they bend the neck of the horse too much to the inside and the shoulders fall out. And because the horse wants to avoid the bending of the joints of the inside hind leg, he happily carries the quarters a little bit to the inside. So it's a chicken or an egg kind of thing. Which is coming first, the horse avoiding the bending and carrying of the weight with the inside hind leg or the riders putting the horse in a position where he cannot be straight because they bend the neck too much and allow the shoulders to fall out? So rather than just give a definition of straightness, I try to make the riders aware of the fact that the shoulders of the horse have to be directly in front of their hips and directly in front of the hips of the horse. If the shoulders are not lined up with the hips then you don't have a horse that is axis straight, and you're part of the problem, not part of the solution.

Jane Savoie

First of all, the rider has to understand the concept of straightness and be straight themselves. If you have a rider who has a crookedness problem, that problem has to be addressed first. This can be done through work on the lunge line for the rider if it's a major crookedness in their body or if they need to separate themselves from the horse and learn what it feels like to be straight without having to worry about the schooling of the horse. Another aid — a visual aid for the rider is watching a video of themselves ride and then maybe watching a more advanced rider ride a similar movement and comparing the two. I find a lot of people can relate to the visual aspect, because if they can't feel what they're doing wrong, they've probably gotten used to being crooked. To change their position and make them straight is very difficult for them so if they can see it, see what they do, see the correct way to ride it, it opens up their ability to feel it more. As for straightness exercises for the horses, lateral exercises help a lot because you can make the horse use themselves more evenly. For example, if you have one side that's stiffer than the other or one side that doesn't track up as much as another. Lateral work also makes the rider more aware of how their aids affect the horse.

Ann Guptill

Whether he's young or old, a green horse isn't straight by nature. As he moves up the levels of dressage, he needs to stay straight in order to gain strength. I think a lot of the crookedness starts to come when you really have to ask them to sit down behind and the weaknesses start to pop out. For instance, even though half-pass is a lateral movement, it still has to be correctly straight. I think that's where you start to see a lot of the crookedness due to the weakness or lack of muscle.

Gwen Blake

What's so important about straightness?

Without straightness, you might just as well not bother to do dressage because without it the horse cannot work properly through, and you can never achieve collection and engagement. You can't achieve the athletic potential of the horse. Severe crookedness in horses due to weakness of the hind leg or severe mental and physical restrictions on one side will mean that horse is not going to make an upper level dressage horse. It takes a good rider to know when the horse is crooked. It takes an even better one not to be too much bothered by it, because all horses are crooked. You can't let that one thing be the focus of your whole work. It isn't. You have many other things to do, not just exercises that are demonstrations of your straightness. It takes a long time to fix crookedness, really a long time, because it is natural and quite likely Mother Nature made it. And it's against Mother Nature to fix it. If it is rider-created, it can be fixed and needs fixing right away by a riding instructor. Even though you've worked on crookedness your whole lifetime on a horse, you can see it when you get to the ultimate test, which is straightness in piaffe, on the centerline, between the reins. You see it expressed now by irregularity. You have one right hind leg that goes further under the body than the left or vice versa. It's very difficult to fix, it's always there, and it always has to be dealt with. It doesn't go away. It's just worked on. Horses are also able to switch stuff. Just when you think you've got it right — look again! It's now on the left side!

Carol Lavell

How do I make my horse straight?

There are so many exercises, and in truth all of the lateral movements that make a horse bend actually teach the horse to be straight, because the ability of a horse to be straight on straight lines and bent on bent lines means that he has to be sufficiently strong and equal in his strength on both sides. So, for instance, if you have a horse that tends to be crooked when he's going to the right and would like to be bent to the left, then part of making him straight is in teaching through using bending exercises to the right to bend his frame. Equally, part of making him be more supple and flexible to the right so he can be straight to the right, is by actually straightening and elongating the left side of the young horse which may want to be hollowed out to the left. We do that by stretching him as he goes around to the right, not reducing the right side of the horse by bending him just by using hand, but by actually elongating the left side of the horse around a long bent right side of the horse. So that by itself is the beginning of straightening the horse. From there at all levels we straighten the horse through the use of exercises like counter-canter and serpentines. Leg-yields are also very helpful in teaching the horse to move straight while going sideways away from the pressure of the leg. Generally, straightness is a quality that comes to the horse over time when the rider has done a good and thorough job in his basic work in the half-halts.

Robert Dover

People don't realize when a horse is crooked, but when you ask them to do an exercise to make the horse straight, they right away get a better balanced feel. They feel more squaring off of the horse's hind legs under their seat. They feel better balanced — the horse is no longer leaning in against centrifugal force or falling away from centrifugal force off the circle. The first thing they say is, "Oh, this feels a whole lot better." The second thing they say is, "It feels so much better balanced on the circle but he's looking to the outside. He doesn't have the right bend. He's not straight."

In truth he's traveling on the circle to the right, his head is slightly to the left, and his right hind leg is slightly to the left and he's actually straight if he were circling left. It's hard for riders to understand that we've made the horse's spine straight even though he's traveling on a circle. That's the second kind of straightness, not straight for the direction you're going, but straight for an exercise you're doing.

Instead of letting the hips go right, you take the right hind leg and put it under the horse's body in front of the other hind leg. And instead of the shoulder going left, you take the nose and neck and you slightly flex and give and bend the horse to the left. Now you take the neck slightly to the left, and the hind leg slightly to the left and still stay on the circle to the right. Now you have a straight horse, but the rider now is terribly worried that the horse isn't bent uniformly going around the circle to the right. I just say in my riding lessons that that's fine with me and maybe next month you get bent to the right but it won't be this month. I don't care how long it takes until the horse is strong enough with the right hind leg, strong enough that the muscles can maintain the bend right on the circle not allowing the shoulder to drift left and the hips right. And it may take a long time. But if the horse is very hard on that right rein, people try very hard to keep taking the right rein away from the horse and flexing and moving the bit, and in the beginning that works. They can take away the right rein, they can give half-halts, they can get the horse a little bit better between the reins and he's not so hard on one rein and against the other rein. After a while the horse gives to the right rein in the neck, doesn't give the poll, doesn't give the jaw, drops behind the bit and he's against the bit at the same time. But the rider gets a better feel on the right rein and the horse has made himself now super crooked. He's behind the bit and to the right with his head and neck and against the bit at the same time and his hips are now usually way over to the left. And so is his shoulder. And the horse bends his neck in front of the withers to the right and takes his whole body away from the right side bending aids. The rider was taught after all to use the right rein and the right leg to bend the horse and she does. And the horse learns to take his whole body and push it more to the outside. Even if he doesn't fall off the circle, he pushed his body outward. And when the rider is supposed to change direction by changing the bend from right to left and go left, the horse immediately comes high and above and against the bit. And the rider wonders what happened to the suppling. It's because the horse never even gave on the right rein in the first place. He just took himself backwards and away from the bit and pushed himself to the left to get away from the correction. It's one of the worst kinds of rider-created crookedness, and I see it every single day when I'm teaching. You have to teach people what that means. They have a better feel on the right rein because they bent the horse a lot to the right when they suppled the neck and jaw on the right. They just don't understand that the horse's body is now bulging so badly to the left, that they're always going to the left in everything the horse does. If a rider is allowed to continue that over a period of months, it becomes a fixed thing in the horse's body and becomes extremely difficult to correct. It's one of the worst things a rider can do to the horse. It takes away his movement, takes away his balance, takes away his ability to do work. The rider has to understand what the horse is doing with his body, and that takes a person on the ground.

I try to get people out of their horse's mouth, because they're trying to control the whole forehand with the reins and yet the reins don't do that. The reins are a communication center in the mouth that communicate to the hind end. They're not for dragging the forehand around. They're to give indications and signals. Riders don't seem to understand that, so I give them an exercise — short turns at the trot, quick turns wavy lines at the trot. and every time the horse tries to fall in and out I won't let the rider touch the reins. I just make them use the legs. And they say they can't turn. That's right, they can't turn, because the horse's hind legs are some place else. Next I allow them to give the half-halts in the new position and then they have to let go of the reins and turn with the leg.

After they've done that for a week, the horse gets off the shoulders, and he

Ann Guptill riding Maple Magnum in passage. Photo by Terri Miller.

knows as you go to turn left, he'd better hurry up and bring his hind leg up underneath himself, because he's just going to get kicked harder. And the rider is not going to help him by pulling on the reins. He has nobody to lean on, no support on the bit, no help. Then the tempo often changes and the rhythm often changes. We don't let the rhythm change, but sometimes the tempo gets slower as the rider tries to turn left. We chase the hind legs right up there and if the horse goes, ouch — can't stand it — it's too bad. He has to learn to use his hind legs. And he's the one that's doing the trotting — not me. I'm just the indicator — turn here, turn here, turn here, too. And hurry up! And don't fall right and don't fall left and I don't correct with the reins; I just give the half-halt and let him go. If he doesn't turn, I kick him harder. It doesn't take long before he's rescuing himself because he's very uncomfortable. This is one way of helping the horse to achieve straightness — hurrying the hind legs up while we're turning; not interfering with the hind legs by pulling on the reins. To achieve straightness in a straight line is reserved for God and Grand Prix horses and that's extremely difficult. So we always do it through bending in lateral work. That's the access to collection and straightness.

We do a lot of counter-suppling with the horse. For instance, tracking right, we put the horse in right shoulder-in on the quarter line, and then we counter-flex to the left and back to the right. The horse thus goes from shoulder-in right to travers left. The shoulders of the horse must never deviate from going forward on the straight line. The key to making the horse straight also means that he allows you to manipulate his body parts. The Training, First and Second Level horse has to be able to look left and travel right and look right and travel left at the walk, trot and canter. On a circle he has to look left when he's going right and look right when he's going left and not shift his body one single degree. If I put the right hind leg to the left on the circle to the right, he has to look left and right without changing that. That means you have control of all the body parts. That means that now when we go in a straighter line, and he tries to shift his weight to get off one hind leg and shift his weight to another and throw his shoulder out so he doesn't have to work with his hind legs under his shoulders we can use these suppling exercises — our legs and our hands — in order to make him straight.

I want to emphasize that you may have a horse who is straight but not for the exercise you're doing. It could be that he has to stay position left with the right hind leg to the left when you're going on a circle to the right, but his tracks will be correct around the circle. His tracks will be on a single track around the circle but he won't have true bend to the right. He is straight in his body not for the exercise you're doing — going around the circle to the right. He isn't yet bent to the right properly, but you are laying the foundation for bend to the right because you're first getting the inside hind legs up under the midline of his abdomen or close to it. In order for him to keep it there, and not fall off the circle, he probably has to look a little to the left. The front end of the horse, the neck and head, is the easiest part of the straightness to correct — not the back end. So having him flex slightly left going around the circle is fine because it helps him control the shoulders and they stay more correctly on the circle. How long do you have to stay there? Who cares — until you can test yourself — you do it for a long time then you finally turn around and say okay, I'm going to take the circle to the right and I am going to have the nose to the right and the shoulders arranged properly on the circle with the outside shoulder ahead, the inside shoulder slightly back and the hips arranged on the circle and I'm traveling on a single track and it's easily balanced and the horse isn't leaning on the reins.

Carol Lavell

Isn't it easy to feel when the horse isn't straight?

What you do habitually feels normal to you. People who have ridden a horse too bent in the neck with the shoulders falling out, think that feels straight. They have to learn a new feeling and what I have them do is flex the horse to the outside — the flexion occurs just at the poll, not in the neck — and feel the shoulders of the horse slide back in front of their hips and in front of the hips of the horse. I have them ride around on circles, through corners, on straight lines in counter-flexion until that placement of the shoulders relative to the hindquarters feels normal to them. The rider must be sure to support with the inside rein so that he has only counter-flexion not counter-bend in the neck. Counter-bend will only make the shoulders fall too much to the inside. That's no better than the shoulders falling out. When that feels normal and not odd anymore, then I allow them to flex the horse correctly in the direction that the horse is bent and strive to keep the shoulders in the same position, not letting them slip to the outside again.

Jane Savoie

Since straightness is a progressive goal, how much straightness can I realistically get at Training and First Levels?

At Training Level, you're just lucky if all the body parts go in the direction you're steering. The amount of time they give to get around the ring between the letters generally is occupied entirely by just trying to keep the horse on some single line, not two tracks, not three tracks, or five tracks. Because the horse's natural tendency is to be crooked, you will travel just like a dog travels, crabbing his way sideways when he's looking back over his shoulders at his master. I mean I don't even take my Training Level horses in a dressage ring anymore, because with my horses I need more room than that to get them thinking straight. I just ride them in a big field and when they get crooked and against on one side, I push them forward to the other side. Straightness is not really possible at Training Level. You spend the whole time thinking about straightness because you are just barely riding the horse forward. When he gets crooked, it's like when a horse trailer tries to wave and sway behind you. The best way to fix the sway is to step on the accelerator and I do that with a horse. As soon as he gets crooked I ride him more forward and maybe the speed is too much for him to handle and he runs on his forehand and loses the rhythm but for me that brief interlude of losing the rhythm and running on his forehand is less important than getting straight. At Training Level the idea is more to bring the hind legs straight toward the shoulders as you instill the idea of going forward to correct the crookedness. Taking more on the reins to correct crookedness can be counterproductive at this stage.

At First Level, you can have more straightness, because at First Level you're thinking of not letting the quarters always be carried in at canter transitions from trot and not letting the horse look in or look out as he pleases. Now you can take more hold of the reins and influence where the head is and the neck is coming out between the shoulders and you are better able to influence where the hips are with your legs because you have taught leg yielding now. He listens to the leg so he can put his body to the left or to the right, and he should be listening to the rein so he can put his neck to the left or the right at First Level. That means that you have a good degree of control of initial straightness. At Training Level, initial straightness was cured by going forward, but not necessarily faster. First Level it's cured by the fact that you've been leg yielding and you have taught the horse to bend his neck left or right when you ask with the hand. But that's about the best you can do because a horse is not balanced enough to do too much more and stay off the forehand. You have to keep in mind the progression of the work in dressage so that the horse becomes straight between the reins and even on the reins. And this is something that takes the horse's lifetime to achieve. It doesn't happen at First, Training or Second or Third Level. If it does, I'd like to know your secret.

Carol Lavell

I am hoping to move up to Second Level this year. How much straightness is achievable at this level?

By Second Level we hope we can trot and walk on circles and on straight lines using the outside rein and coming forward from the inside leg and keeping the outside leg steady behind the girth to control the horse from shifting away from the inside suppling rein.

By Second Level you are able to use real dressage aids. If you've been training in the classical way — you've taught the horse to go in position, you've taught the horse about shoulder-fore. You are now able to move the hindquarters and neck to the right and to the left. Now you will find that the most difficult part to manipulate is the shoulder, since, if you can move the shoulder this implies a large degree of balance off the forehand. A supple horse is just like a roll of pennies that you get from the bank in that brown wrapper. You open up the wrapper and try to push the roll of pennies across the table in that little roll, and they all start to fall left and right and finally, like a Slinky, they just all fall off. That's what a First Level horse entering Second Level is like unless he's very stiff in which case he's usually crooked but very connected, meaning that his body parts are not flying in all different directions. They are stuck together with such rigidity that they're always in one direction only. That kind of horse is actually easier to ride straight on a line than a supple horse. People

Bent Jensen with Royalist at the extended trot. Photo by M. Cabell.

always want supple horses, but they're very difficult to keep arranged.

Entering Second Level you're starting shoulder-in, an exercise I don't believe should ever be started without collection. At Training Level and First Level, I get the correct angle and the number of tracks — three, and I even get bend. The thing that is not correct is the impulsion, and the amount of engagement needed for the horse to lift his shoulders up with his hindquarters. Therefore, I am now actually teaching crookedness in the horse. He's not straight for the direction he's supposed to be traveling in which is correct. The lack of straightness that shows up is the part that the horse's neck is pulled to the inside. The rider then takes the inside leg and shoves the horse to the outside so that he doesn't fall in when they pull the neck in, and he stays on the track with his quarter or away from the track with his quarters off to the outside and they bend the neck in, and the outside shoulder sticks out on the track. And now we have maybe three tracks but the horse has moved away from the inside leg, instead of being bent around it, and that's incorrect. The horse's neck is now stuck over against the inside shoulder blade, and the horse is not free to move forward and up toward the bit and neither is the inside hind leg free to engage toward the inside of the bridle and therefore the horse is now very crooked. And so the more you try shoulder-in at Second Level the more crooked the rider makes the horse. As a judge, practically everything I see at Second Level is crooked and incorrectly done. It seems to me it might be inappropriate to do shoulder-in at this level without true collection and it's hard to get that.

Carol Lavell

What does straightness have to do with collection?

Unless both hind legs work really closely together up underneath the horse's abdomen toward his shoulders, the hind legs cannot lift his body up off the ground in the front. The front legs merely get out of the way of the hind legs. The front legs do not lift the horse — the hind legs do, connected by that hammock called the back. The mouth is just the power steering. It's not the thing that lifts the horse but you see riders trying to do it all the time with their hands. And so you have to have the hind legs under the that they are going to lift — and not out behind it — not to the left, not to the right. In the meantime when you put those hind legs under there, if a shoulder tries to go to the left or the right, you lose it. And that's why he cannot be collected unless he's straight. He has to have both hind legs working at full power right underneath there. This kind of collection is not achievable until nearly FEI. And yet we have judges in this country saying that collection at Second and Third Level is the same as collection at Grand Prix, when we all know as trainers that's impossible. The people who slow down horses in order to gain collection because they know that the speed of collected trot is slower in miles per hour than medium or extended, are on the wrong track entirely. Slower speed does not, can not, make collection. It's speedy, weight-accepting hind legs under the horse's body that make collection. And they have to be very quick to answer the leg (those are speedy hind legs) and the horses have to be very good in the mouth, neck and jaw. The rider has to tend to both things at once between First Level and Third. He has to learn that at that moment of giving, to really put the hind legs up. You do this with the whip if you need to — even if the horse runs a little bit — and then pat him. If you don't go through this bad situation, chances are by the time you get to Third Level he won't be able to do it. You cannot miss the opportunity. If he doesn't learn to use his hind legs before he is seven years old, teaching him is not going to be easy. I don't mean using his hind legs like Grand Prix but he has to discover that he has a pair and start to learn what they're for. It's too late after this time to teach them what they're for.

Carol Lavell

Walk Work

Q I know the walk is important, but I often overlook it. What are the characteristics of a good working walk?

In a correct working walk we see:

1. Energy
2. Regularity
3. Some degree of overstep

There is sufficient energy in the walk if it is easy for the horse to lengthen the stride when asked. The walk is regular if there is even spacing between the four steps of each stride. The sequence of legs in the walk is outside hind, outside fore, inside hind, inside fore. You should be able to count an even 1-2-3-4 rhythm rather than, for instance, 1-2...3-4. There should be some degree of overstep depending on the innate athletic ability of the horse.

You can probably ruin the walk more easily than any of the other gaits so I am reluctant to work a young horse a lot on contact and very careful when introducing collection in the walk because you always want to preserve the purity of the gait. Especially with the bigger movers, the longer the natural overstride, the more careful you have to be. I've found for walks that degenerate and tend to get a little impure sometimes riders can try to slow the walk and make the rhythm more even that way. Another way I've found helpful is to go sideways — to do a leg yield until the rhythm becomes regular, straighten the horse and for as many steps as he maintains that good rhythm, allow him to stay straight. As soon as the rhythm degenerates push him sideways so he learns to walk in a better rhythm.

Jane Savoie

What you look for in a good walk is four distinct beats with an overstep, which means that his hind foot will fall distinctly in front of the step of the front foot on the same side. Now that is a scenario that would be perfect. The most important thing I would say is that the horse makes always four very distinct beats in the walk — that when the horse is landing with the left hind leg, for instance, the left foreleg should just be coming off the ground. You want that timing between each step. When you have a horse that is too long in his overstride, that can be equally dangerous as the horse that has too short a stride or no overstride, because usually the horse that has an enormous overstride does so by not bending the joints of the hind legs when he walks. And that's the horse that will have the danger of coming to a lateral walk or pace as he's collected and have trouble coming to a collected walk where the horse should just barely move into the hoofprint on the same side with his hind foot and be able to come to a balance where he lowers his croup and walks with energy in that same four-beat walk.

Robert Dover

The walk is the most difficult gait, because there is no engagement. Working walk should be in the same frame as the working trot. If the horse tends to shorten too much or feel constrained, having a little longer frame to maintain a four-beat, relaxed walk is recommended. The contact with the rein may be lighter because there is not the power from the hind leg. It is important to feel the rhythm of the walk. Not so quick that the rider cannot feel the legs, but not sluggish, feeling like the horse is in molasses.

A good way to tell if the horse is in working walk is if he steps directly into working trot when asked. If the walk is short and up and down the horse will go into a short choppy trot at first. If the walk is a medium or free walk, the first steps will either be short to catch his balance, or he will step off in a long free trot.

Pam Goodrich

There seems to be a lot of controversy as to when the collected walk can be safely started and how it should look. Can you clarify?

As a judge, I have a conviction about the collected walk, and I know it is controversial, but I also know it is shared by some well respected horsemen and judges. I consider the collected walk a movement, not a gait. To me, there is nothing natural about a collected walk, and although I may score a collected walk that has poor rhythm or is a clear pace as "insufficient" or less, I will not penalize the horse in the general impressions for gaits unless he also shows the same problems in the extended walk. Too many times, I have seen horses showing an extended walk worthy of a seven or even an eight, only to turn into a four as soon as he is asked to collect. In my opinion, it is not appropriate to penalize him twice for the same "crime," since the extended walk is a genuine gait.

Anne Gribbons

The collected walk is a touchy movement to ride because it depends less on what you're doing while you are riding it than it does on what balance and self-carriage the horse has already achieved. The collected walk should be active. The hind leg should be behind or just in the footfall of the front leg, but it must be an active, marching gait. A lot of what I see in the show ring in this country today is too fast, and that's the most common mistake.

Gary Rockwell

I don't do any collected walk with a young horse. I just leave it as a working walk.

Gwen Blake

What can be done to improve a horse's walk?

I have found that the easiest gait to improve is the trot, the canter can be quite tricky, and the walk is a royal pain. The reason for this appears to be that in the absence of thrust and impulsion it is much harder to impress the horse with the driving aids, and also easier for the animal to evade by getting behind the aids, above the aids and crooked. If the rider pushes too hard, the horse tends to break into a trot or lose the clear four-beat. If the rider leaves him alone, he tends to shuffle and drag until one diagonal in a test feels a week long. It takes experience and a good natural "feel" to ride the walk to its potential.

Anne Gribbons

Normally the young horse stays either on a long contact in the walk or will work in a medium walk but we won't go to collected walk until the horse is already sufficiently working in collected trot and collected canter. There's nothing wrong with working in the walk. People tend to stay away from the walk. They think, oh my God, if I start working in the walk I'm going to diminish the walk — I'm going to ruin it. The truth is that working in the walk can make for a much more successful training career for the horse and can teach him a lot of the ideas that he has to know to be able to achieve the same kinds of flexibility and the same kinds of movements and balances in the trot and canter. So I would encourage riders to work in the walk every day, to make a part of their workout working in what we call the medium or working walk, the free walk on a long rein or extended walk when we come to Second Level and higher. The horse with a poor walk definitely needs to work in the walk.

Robert Dover

What are some of the common problems encountered in walk work?

The biggest problem with many very young horses is that they are not yet strong enough to take a real contact in the walk. There's no suspension at the walk and there is less forward momentum than in the trot and the canter so they don't have the push and the carry that they have in the trot and canter. To avoid problems, I ask all my riders with lower level horses to do lengthenings in the walk and medium walks, hardly ever asking for a working walk. That way the horses are encouraged to stay forward and reaching into the reins in the walk.

Ann Guptill

I can never do a free walk across the diagonal without my horse snatching at the reins. What am I doing wrong?

Usually a lack of steadiness and a lack of carriage through their back causes horses to do this. They have to be sent forward. They snatch the reins because they don't want to stay connected through their back onto the rein from the hind leg, and the snatching of the reins is either to relieve their back or to get the riders to let go of the reins. So the rider has to keep a steady hand and kick him right back forward into the reins.

Ann Guptill

Usually there are two reasons. One is tension and the other is disobedience. The tension can mean many things. It can just be his temperament as in the case of some Thoroughbreds. It can be due to fear. He may be afraid that when the rein is given it is going to be taken back and he wants to get away from it. Or, the disobedient horse says, "good, I'm done, let me have this rein — my rein. Give it to me!" In both instances though, the correction is pretty much the same and that is that when you relax your arm forward to give the rein, you don't let the rein slide. You actually do it by relaxing your arm forward so that if the horse snatches the rein, you don't have an open hand so that the horse can get the rein away. The second thing is that I do it with an open rein so if the horse does snatch, he'll hit my hand but it's not in a backwards action. The snatch will be felt on the corner of the mouth which will hopefully be strong enough that it discourages him but not backwards so that he bounces back away from the reins. The most important thing is that the rider must maintain an elastic contact regardless of what the horse does. That way the horse learns that he can't get away from the rein, and he can't take the rein away from the rider.

Pam Goodrich

I've been noticing that my horse is beginning to have a lateral walk. What causes this and how can I fix it?

I think this is a very serious problem and very difficult to really correct many times. I think the only thing you can do is do lateral work at the walk and sometimes that helps because it sort of breaks up the rhythm for the horse to do haunches-in or half-pass. Actually I do quite a bit of work at the walk where I'll go from half-pass into shoulder-in. That really keeps the horse listening to the inside leg. I find that sometimes helps a problem in the walk, but not always.

Charlotte Bredahl

If the horse has a lateral walk, then you work in that walk by trying to dissect the walk into its four beats. You can do that by halting and then walking off. And always note that the first step that you achieve in the horse as he walks off will be his best step. So if you can basically gauge what it is you're feeling when you take that first step, and then try to retain that to the second step, then to the third step and so forth, you'll find that you're achieving a better walk with each day that you work on it.

Robert Dover

A lot of times what I do is ride him just a little bit slower in the walk, but keep pushing the hind end under by doing lateral movements within the walk.

Gwen Blake

Anything you can do to break up the sequence. Sometimes slight shoulder-in will help — shoulder-in at the walk, a little bit, or making the horse hesitate. In other words, every time he starts getting a little lateral and quick, make a brief halt, and then let him walk on and then a brief halt and let him walk on. You can do that also

Carol Lavell and Gifted, at the extended trot. Photo courtesy of the USET.

in the shoulder-in where you make a little shoulder-in and make him wait and then go on and then wait.

Jessica Ransehousen

You'll often see this with the horse that doesn't have a good quality walk by nature or that has learned how to back off the rider a little when they've picked him up. I find that by putting the horse in a lateral or bending position, you can often get him out of the pacing walk. Again, I use the turn on the forehand to get them to take the contact and may also pick them up into the collected or working walk using the shoulder-fore.

Ann Guptill

If the horse has a lateral walk by nature or if a horse is tending to be lateral, you're better off not to do very much walk work with him on contact in his early training, but instead, concentrate on relaxation. Lateral walks can be caused by a rider who is pushing with or stiffening his back, or not following the motion of the horse very well with his upper body or by a hand that is interfering or never really following the motion of the horse.

Gary Rockwell

A pacey or lateral walk is difficult to correct, so it's important to prevent it. One should avoid buying a horse that has a tendency for lateralness, which can be hereditary or trained in from tenseness. I do not work young horses very much in the working walk, and not at all in the collected walk. To keep the naturalness and freedom of the walk, it is good to walk outside in the woods, fields or trails, not always in the arena. Whether it is my young horses or FEI horses, I take them on a walk hack before and after schooling.

A good correction for a lateral walk is to ride shoulder-in, at the correct walk rhythm and tempo, not too fast and not restrictive in the reins. The rider must be able with this type of horse to ride the walk rhythm with his seat, and not to be adjusting the horse in the reins.

When a horse has a good walk, then it is good to do suppling work in the walk, because it helps to keep the back loose. For example, on the long side, to alternate from shoulder-in to travers, or shoulder-in to renvers. Another example would be to begin the diagonal in the leg yield, change the bend to half-pass, and then change the bend to leg yield again. Done properly with good half-halts, this exercise will help to keep the shoulders and back loose.

Kathy Connelly

I can't seem to get a good half-pirouette. What's the secret?

Half pirouettes at the walk are correctly performed when the horse maintains the rhythm of the walk and the engagement, remains on the aids and on steady contact, keeps the activity of the inside hind leg (does not swivel on the inside foot) and moves straight forward when the turn is complete. An even bend in the direction of the turn will put the finishing touch to the ideal picture. Common faults are: horse above the aids, resisting the bend, inside leg sticking, haunches falling out, loss of walk rhythm, turning on the center, backing in the turn, and over-turning, i.e., going past 180 degrees.

The cure for almost all of these faults is proper preparation. This is true for every movement performed, but there's no faking it or "getting lucky" at the walk. If the horse is not well in front of the leg and firmly on the aids, he will shut off behind and hollow his back just when you need him most. If the horse has a clear four-beat walk, is well in hand and attentive to the driving aids, a slight shoulder-in position (just think it) for a step or two immediately before the start of the turn helps to activate the inside hind leg and confirm the connection with the outside rein. The rider's weight has to stay on the inside seatbone throughout the turn to help the horse balance, and his inside leg maintains the engagement, while the outside leg "directs" the turn and prevents the hindquarters from escaping to the outside.

Anne Gribbons

A half-pirouette in the walk is an 180 degree half turn with the hind legs stepping up and down practically on the spot and the forehand prescribing a half circle around them. The horse should be bent in the direction he is turning and maintain a four beat walk.

I train walk pirouettes very similarly to the way I train canter pirouettes. I do schooling walk pirouettes which are large enough that the hind legs don't stick. I put the horse in the position I want, meaning slightly bent to the inside, and I apply the aids. I use my inside leg at the girth for the bend and to keep the inside hind leg going, and my outside leg a little back to hold the hind leg from stepping wide. The outside rein is the main rein that brings the horse's shoulders around. I stay there, however many revolutions it takes, until the horse figures out how to move the hind legs little and the front legs big in a walk rhythm without stumbling and falling down. I don't come out of it until they've done two or three strides that are like a turn on the haunches, meaning not quite on the spot but very regular, very easy. The horse says, "I know where to go within the confines of these aids." And I do that until I can walk on a straight line and one stride before I just sit a little bit lighter and tighter just to say, "Shorten up a little bit." Then I put those aids on, and the horse should know how to stay within those confines from doing all of the schooling pirouettes. I do a half-pirouette, and if it's not good, I keep going around until he does it. That way the horse learns that he can't get out of a half-pirouette.

Pam Goodrich

What are some of the common faults in the half-pirouette?

I'd rather talk about turn on the haunches first because that, in my mind, is a more systematic progression. It's a way to avoid getting into trouble with your half-pirouette because it is a preliminary exercise to pirouettes. The major differences are that half-turns on the haunches are done in the working walk while half-pirouettes are done in the collected walk. In the half-turn on the haunches, the horse is allowed to make a very small circle with the hindlegs about the size of a dinner plate whereas in the half-pirouette the horse should be doing it pretty much on the spot. The common denominator is that the rhythm of the walk must be maintained. As far as schooling is concerned, it is better to err on the side of making these turns too large. You want to avoid putting the horse in a position where it's so difficult that he has to pivot on a hind leg, swing hindquarters out, or lose bend. Teach him the good qualities that go into the turn and sacrifice the size in the beginning.

Jane Savoie

The most common fault is not picking up one hind leg (sticking). Some horses do even worse and pivot on both hindlegs, meaning keeping both hindlegs on the ground and pivoting around them. The best thing to do is large continuous turns on the haunches with encouraging leg or whip to make sure the horse is not allowed to stop with his hindlegs.

Often horses step out with their hindlegs and turn more around their center. These horses need to do large turns on the haunches in haunches-in to gain obedience to the outside leg.

Some horses come around too quickly, falling on their inside shoulder and spinning around. The rider should try to do the half-pirouette with more bend and inside leg. Often doing a quarter turn — going straight — then another quarter turn will gain obedience to the inside aids. Or, they step out with their hind legs and do a turn around the center. Or, they make it so big that they don't have to work hard.

Pam Goodrich

Loss of energy — that's number one. People have this idea that they're going to stop and turn, and they lose their hind end, or they just stop walking and they pivot — or they do what I call a turn around the middle, and the hind end is falling out — way out. I find the best way to correct that is to have people do a half-pass first and then say okay, now do a quarter turn and then half-pass again because you always see people lose the bend. But if you go half-pass, quarter turn into half-pass, it forces the rider to put the inside leg back on to get back into the half-pass. And then sometimes I'll have them do quarter turn and then leg yield back to where they came from, again, for the riders to keep the inside leg on and for the horse to keep active on the inside hind.

Charlotte Bredahl

The degree of collection increases quite a bit as the horse moves up the levels. The tightness of the pirouette is very important as he advances. He has to be able to maintain the activity behind and keep stepping all the way through on a smaller pirouette which requires more strength for him to carry. The rhythm has to stay exactly the same, and the frame has to stay the same. A lot of times in lower levels you see horses wanting to swing out if their rider tries to make a "more advanced pirouette." The suppleness isn't quite there so you usually don't have quite enough bending or a lot of times you have the horse falling down on the forehand in the walk pirouette — the poll suddenly drops down and the horse tries to escape that way.

Gwen Blake

CHAPTER 6

Trot Work

I am starting at Second Level where collected trot is first required. What are the characteristics of a collected trot properly performed?

In the collected trot you want to see what Germans call *schwung*. That is the ability to swing in the back with powerful engaged hind legs and the ability to change the balance at the will of the rider to produce more engagement and, when necessary, to be able to have the scope to then push from that collection towards extension. In collected trot, you're looking for the animal who maintains a perfect balance and a harmony, a beautiful arched neck with the poll being raised and the carriage bringing the head close to the vertical. The collected trot, I believe, should always show the extension within it. So when I talk to my riders I say always feel extension in collection and collection by extension and that's how you know that the horse is truly collected. Only when you feel the ability to produce anything else, whether that be extended trot, halt, collected canter, passage, do you really and truly have a totally collected trot.

Robert Dover

The rhythm is essential and the hind legs must be stepping forward. That they can keep the same rhythm in the collected trot and the medium trot and, hopefully, the extended trot. But the hind legs must still track up in the collected trot. Too often the frame shortens, but the hind leg also shortens.

Ann Guptill

Even in the Grand Prix, the collected trot should be a big trot. I have always felt that people get the idea when they begin collected work at Second Level that now it's time to shorten and make smaller. In fact, although at those middle levels, you're trying through collecting movements and transition work to achieve a collected balance, you want to think "active" and not "small." A Third Level collected trot is still a big forward trot. If you see the L and M tests in Europe, the horses are really going forward but with engagement and balance. You have to be achieving a balance as you go through the levels while always maximizing the horse's gait at the same time so that when you get to Grand Prix, your horse has a big movement.

Gary Rockwell

What's essential for a good collected trot is that the horse is carrying himself, and he's active, and he's round and balanced. That can vary in accordance with the type of movement that the horse has.

Belinda Nairn

That he can be so supple and narrow his hind legs so well that the collection becomes not something you brought from the front end, but from the hind end.

Carol Grant Oldford

The judges always write that there's not enough difference between my trot lengthening and my working trot. Why do I have this problem?

Sometimes people are so afraid the horses are going to get on the forehand that they try to shorten them up, and rather than letting them lengthen the neck, they shorten the neck in. And then the horse will just learn to run rather than stretch over the top line and move forward. In the beginning many people try to do a whole long side or a whole diagonal, and I think that's a mistake. I like to do just a few steps and then back, and make the horse come back and sit down and then go forward again a few steps and then back again. I do this maybe two or three times on the long side rather than trying to go across the diagonal. I don't lengthen all the way across until they're doing it really well for a few steps at a time. In the beginning I always do it in a pretty long frame.

Charlotte Bredahl

How does one go about developing the medium and extended trots?

If a horse has a weak or flat trot, one thing I have found to really help for medium and extended trot is a very steep leg yielding — not the kind of leg yielding that you would want to do in a show, but really making a horse cross over with an exaggerated bending. Make the leg yield from the corner from K right over to B or even reach the track before B so the horse has to really cross over and bend. Then when you reach the track, send them on a little bit, still using a little bit of the concept of leg yielding in the lengthening. When you ask him to lengthen, put your inside leg on and keep the inside rein a little bit so you can maintain activity and suppleness. This seems to increase the stride and allow more suspension through their back.

Belinda Nairn

We've used a lot of trot poles. Renard, the horse that I recently showed Fourth Level, always had a huge big trot but couldn't carry himself in that big a trot. He covered too much ground for the amount of rhythm that he could hold. I did a lot of trotting poles with him starting out with short distances — about four feet, spreading them gradually to five feet, then going to raised cavalletti to teach him to hold himself in the air in a good rhythm. This type of trot work helped him develop a good medium trot.

Ann Guptill

The medium and extended trots grow out of the collected trot just as the lengthening grows out of the working trot. By definition, a lengthening is somewhat on the forehand because a working gait is, relatively speaking, on the forehand. If your mediums and extensions grow out of collection, which they should, you should maintain that feeling of collection in the upper gears. Therefore you have a feeling of going up a hill like an airplane taking off or a speed boat in the water. When that lightness of the forehand is maintained, it is very exciting to watch.

Jane Savoie

CHAPTER 7

Canter Work

Q What are the characteristics of a good working canter?

A good canter must be distinctly three-beat, must have the ability to collect and go on the spot, retaining that three-beat rhythm, and also retaining a great degree of harmony and balance. I look for a canter with a certain amount of knee action because I think that it shows more expression as I do also in the trot a bit. It produces better marks when you move out to extended canter and when you show the flying changes. The collected canter is of great importance because so much of the test is performed within the collected canter. The zigzags in Grand Prix, the flying changes, the medium and extended canters, the pirouettes. Having ridden horses that didn't have great canters I know how important it is to have one.

Robert Dover

Q No matter what I do, I can't seem to push my horse out of a four-beat canter. What causes this problem and is there anything I can do about it?

A horse that has a four-beat canter from the very beginning usually has it because of conformation, an inability to engage its hind legs sufficiently. In some instances, it has to do with the breed of the horse. You can't expect, for instance, a Tennessee Walking Horse to canter the way a German Hanoverian would canter, generally. The sequence of footfalls in the canter is: outside hind leg, then you have the inner hind leg and outer foreleg, and last the inner foreleg. A four-beat canter occurs when the diagonal pair (the inner hind leg and the outer foreleg) don't hit the ground at the exact same second. Normally this has to do with a lack of engagement and a lack of balancing within the horse that would allow his inner hind leg to stay up off the ground until the outer foreleg is able to hit the ground with it. Usually you'll see that with a fallen type of back — the back has fallen away from the rider at that second. Many times this will also occur with stiffening in the neck and in the jaw of the horse. To some degrees, my horse Romantico had a poor canter. When I first got him in '82, his canter was very difficult, very flat, verging on four beats. He had an inability to bend the high joints in his hind leg and the hip and the stifle sufficiently to lower his croup to be able to raise the wither and the shoulders up so that he could have a nice airy three-beat canter. So, what I did was to take him out of collection and back to the idea of medium and extended canter. I did this riding him on a race track for a long time. I made sure that he stayed very round and very deep in his canter, and I kept driving him in the medium and extended canter where he did have a three-beat canter until I was able to reduce in increments the size of the canter stride while maintaining the jump of the canter to keep that three-beat feeling. And so over time it improved enough that he was finally able to make an Olympic team. The best thing you can do for a horse that has a problem in his canter is use exercises within the canter such as medium canter to small circles, which forces the horse to engage. This is how you help the horse achieve the goal you have for him as opposed to getting frustrated and then trying to force him with your strength. It's his strength that he lacks, not his will.

Robert Dover

Lateral work helps — half-passes in the canter — suppling exercises, transition work forward and back. The rider must give the horse a chance to move well in the canter with a following hand and a relaxed back. You have to have a good sense of rhythm yourself in order to try to influence the horse to develop three-beats.

Gary Rockwell

The sequence of legs in the canter is outside hind, that's your strike-off leg, and then the diagonal pair inside hind and outside fore and lastly, the leading leg and then there is a period of suspension. The fourth beat comes when that diagonal pair splits a little bit. Once again we have to be concerned whether it's a rider-created problem or whether by nature the horse doesn't have a good canter. The answer of what to do is obvious if it's a rider problem, such as a restrictive contact. For the horse, I find that if you do a lot of lengthening and shortening or transitions, it will improve the gait in much the same way as going sideways in the walk did. Do something that helps the horse learn how to go in a better rhythm. And it is going to be different for different horses, so in one case lengthening and shortening may help you find the rhythm, while in another case shoulder-fore or frequent canter-walk transitions might help you find the rhythm. Do something that helps the individual horse find a clear rhythm.

Jane Savoie

Several reasons for the four-beat canters can be that the rider has attempted to collect the horse before he is strong enough to hold the frame or he has been put into too short a frame, or he's been ridden from the front to the back rather than the back to the front so his neck has gotten short and his back flat and he loses rhythm behind. They're usually very strong into the hands when they're doing this. This is another concept the riders have to understand: they have to be able to ride the hind leg forward even if the horses are getting strong up front. If they lose the rhythm, most riders tend to want to take back rather than go forward.

Ann Guptill

Here again I'd go back to the exercise that I school in preparing the horse for pirouettes and collection, and that is to bring a horse back to the hindquarters, quicken the hind legs and move him forwards — a lot of forward and back movement to help bring the horse up off his forehand and make him stay active behind.

Gwen Blake

How do you start teaching the horse to lengthen in the canter?

The first thing you have to think about is maintaining rhythm. If you have a good rhythm during the lengthening, then chances are you're going to have a decent transition back. Riders tend to rush the horses a little so first I tell them to think about big, ground-covering bounds so that they don't feel like they're in a hurry and they don't chase him beyond his rhythm. There are a lot of things to do to help this transition back to the working canter, and to help give the horse the idea that the balance should not degenerate. Whatever degree of collection that you have as you go into it, you should have at least that, and no less, as you finish. For instance, come through the corner in a little shoulder-fore, straighten the horse, do your big ground-covering bounds and in the transition back put the horse in shoulder-fore because it's a collecting exercise. A lot of times the horses are not schooled to be obedient enough to the half-halt at the end of the lengthening and the rider has to be too strong with the hands. In this case it could be helpful before you start your lengthenings to do canter-halt, canter-halt, canter-halt or canter-walk, canter-walk

Belinda Nairn on Disney at the extended trot. Photo by Terri Miller.

transitions with the same combination of aids — your seat, your upper legs, your outside rein — that you're going to use to bring the horse back from the lengthening. As a result what you're asking him to do when you go from lengthening to shortening is already in his repertoire. Then ride the half-halt with the same combination of aids that you used for the down transitions. Schooled in this way, you can do a tactful half-halt at the end of your lengthening. You won't have to be too strong which can stop the hind legs causing the horse to stiffen or break to the trot.

Jane Savoie

You lengthen in degrees so that you prevent the horse from losing his balance, but you produce more and more suppleness and agility and you ask for the lengthening again and again. We do an exercise on a 20-meter circle riding a half-halt as you go by the centerline and then on the open part of the circle, you ask the horse to lengthen for some strides. If the horse lost his balance you could bring him back and produce either a ten or 15-meter circle again and then go on with it. This is done in a positive way. When you feel like you've achieved lengthening on the 20-meter circle, you can go off that and do a half of a long side with a lengthening, making sure that you keep the forehand straight in front of the hindquarters and don't allow the haunches to come in. By the middle letter you might ride onto a 12 or 15-meter circle or on a First Level 4 horse you would do a ten meter circle. That helps the animal learn that when he's brought back, he has to think of engaging his hind legs in order to achieve some balance. So rather than really pulling backward, use the circle to help the horse and yourself achieve the balance so that he learns that at the end of the lengthening we have a small circle — and he'd better be ready for it.

Robert Dover

We've been starting canter lengthenings down the long side, but my horse either takes off or gets so heavy I can't pick him back up. It feels like he's going to gallop right out of the arena.

Generally they're going to tip over and get down on their forehand. As they start to tip down, take the outside rein and circle away, depending on the level of the horse and his balance, make a ten or 15-meter circle, put him back on the wall in shoulder-fore, and ask him to go forward. When he starts to go down in front and run, take the outside rein and turn him with the outside rein again until when you ask him to go forward, he goes forward in balance.

Crookedness and loss of rhythm are the problems. The rider must use shoulder-fore so that the horse learns to canter straight, because almost all horses will normally canter in haunches-in. If the horse has a really good canter rhythm they can get crooked and still keep the rhythm. Usually if they get crooked, they're going to run in the lengthening and lose the rhythm instead of going forward in the lengthening.

Ann Guptill

When a horse gets heavy in the lengthening he is generally coming too low in his shoulders and keeping his croup high, causing him to lose his rhythm. This is due to too much weight coming onto the forehand and the fact that he is not responding to the collecting aids. A good exercise is to practice five or six strides of lengthening-collect with proper half halts and make an eight or ten meter circle re-establishing the horse's balance and straightness.

Canter-walk-canter transitions are excellent to improve his ability to maintain his weight on his hind end and to engage. A horse that is green in his training or weak in his back muscles will tend to want to bring his haunches in. It is important with these horses to ride the short side and corners of the arena in shoulder fore to have them straight before embarking on the long side in a canter lengthening.

Kathy Connelly

My horse either falls into a trot or falls on his face when lengthening down the long side. How do I teach him to stay together?

They'll usually trot because they've dropped or stiffened their back, gotten long and strung out, or lost their balance. Doing a whole long side in lengthened canter is often too much for the green horse. A good exercise is to ride a 20-meter circle in the center of the ring, first riding him forward a few strides and then coming back and repeating this around the circle until the rider can feel the rhythm, and maintain the balance. Then take this exercise off the circle and down the long side asking a few strides of lengthenings at a time until the horse can hold his balance in lengthening.

Ann Guptill

How do you start developing the medium and extended canters?

This needs to be done not on long diagonals or on long sides. It needs to be done for short distances, a few strides forward, a few strides back. I like to do it on a very large circle — 20-meter and larger. And the important thing is not that the horse makes a medium or extended canter for a long period, but that he displays a readiness to go forward and a willingness to come back. If he becomes really ready to go from your aids and ready to come back from your aids, then you can always do a whole diagonal.

Gary Rockwell

One, the rider has to let the horse go. By the time they get to developing medium and extended canters, I find that most riders are trying to hold the horse round with the reins, but he doesn't stay round and on the bit. As soon as they go forward, he comes beyond, above and against the bit. Many horses, when you go bigger, become harder, tighter, shorter in the neck and come behind the vertical and against the bit. What I do first, is to give the horse the desire, (which is generally lacking here, because the rider has been pulling on the reins so much) to gallop and be free. I supple and give and make the horse good in the neck and the jaw. As soon as he gives a little, I give the reins and send him off with a whip and a leg. The whip is an aid, not a punishment. I cluck and he runs away and I pat him before I take the reins back, because his head is now in the air. I pat him to say that he did a good job, because he went. Then I carefully take back the reins and put things right in the front. I supple him and until he's nice and soft in the reins, a few steps, then I give the rein away and ask him to go again. After ten of those strides the horse stops running away and he starts to go in a more relaxed way. He's expecting the pat at the end and expecting the soft suppling and he's not grabbed by the rider and put back together, and he's allowed to go.

Carol Lavell

I start on the long side and ride shoulder-fore and change tempo until we are in an extended canter. After that I go on the diagonal. Usually I don't have any problem, but if I do, then I go back and do it on the long side the same way.

Bent Jensen

What is the most common problem you see with riders trying to teach their horse medium and extended canter?

Most of the trouble I see with riders doing medium and extended is that they're pulling and giving half-halts and fooling around with the reins, trying to keep him round the whole time and together and off his forehand with the reins. The horses get more and more stilted, the legs more and more lateral. The inside legs land together and go forward together, they lose the regularity of the gait. My way of fixing this is to make the rider ease the reins away and they hate it, because they have no control. And it's awful to begin with. It's the worst stuff you ever saw. The riders have no control, the horses are afraid — someone let go of the reins, and now they're afraid when the reins are taken back that they're going to get hurt. They're waiting to get grabbed and get that half-halt. It doesn't take them too long to settle down. Then the next thing is that when the horse is free to go, they usually start to stretch toward the bit, which is a joy to see. Now that they are going, all I have to do is get it under a little control. The first rule of dressage riding is that you're not allowed to pull on the reins until the horse is going, not allowed to take the bit backwards away from the horse. That should have been learned at Training Level. For some reason people forget it in medium and extended. Why they drop the idea of going first before they do that with the rein I don't know. It's gone from the rider's curriculum. At first I don't focus on roundness, connection, shoulder-fore. Go. They don't have to go far, but they have to go from the leg. So we do that and then we take back the bit carefully and we send them again and then they start to relax and they offer to go now. You'll see the improvement right away, because they become relaxed in the neck and jaw and that cleans up the regularity right away.

Carol Lavell

How do you maintain straightness in medium and extended canter?

Crookedness ruins a really good quality medium and extended, because it makes the horse flat when he tries to push aside to the right or push aside to the left. You still have to have a degree of flexion even though you're going straight across the diagonal in medium or extended. Without it you don't have quality. It is a gait where one side is slightly longer than the other. Even though it doesn't look that way, it feels that way when you're riding. If the horse is too curled around that inside leg, he may have to be put in a slight counter-flexion while traveling in a straight line. You have to insist that the horse stay on the correct lead now. The first thing that happens is that the horse falls to the right. Most of them do. You're not allowed to take the reins so you use the right leg to support him toward the left rein even though you don't use very much of it, and he switches leads. He switches through resistances and stiffness. I have tried putting the horse in haunches-in or even half-pass for the down transition when he switches leads. My best success has been not to mind when they switch — just put them back on the lead and do it again and again and again. Unless it's a really stupid horse, when he's changed back for the 53rd time in one lesson, he starts to get the idea that he has to stay there. I make the rider lean over to the inside and stay on the inside. The horse doesn't want them to stay there. I make the rider stay there and use the inside leg in the down transition and keep the horse on the outside rein, not only with the outside hand but with the outside and inside legs together. And yes, the horse will change a thousand times in lesson; but eventually he'll start to stay on the outside rein even if you don't have much of it. He'll start to learn and you'll start to get a better quality canter, but you have to live through that unfortunate stage where he's switching. And you cannot correct in a strong way. You just put the horse back on the lead and keep doing it until he listens to the inside leg.

Carol Lavell

I have a problem with my horse becoming lateral in the extended and medium canter.

It's pretty common with a bad canter for the horse's inside hind and inside front leg to be trying to strike the ground at the same time. I have a horse who paced in the down transition for two years. We had a good extended canter, and every time I touched the reins to make collected canter, he paced. The best way to clean up rhythm is, if the hind leg is early, meaning the horse is overridden with the leg, and the front legs are back a little bit, to delay the hind leg by putting the horse in shoulder-in. We take the inside hind leg and instead of making it travel straight forward where it gets early, overridden by the rider, we place it towards the outside of the movement, meaning that the right hind leg will go to the left if you're on the right lead. Doing this delays the path, delays the flight time and delays the landing time, because the horse is in flight time to the outside with the inside hind leg.

The horse that leans over on the bit is in charge of the bit. That kind of horse I don't ever let approach the bit. I take it away from him by moving the bit in his mouth and as soon as he gives, I tap him with the whip to chase his hind legs a little until he no longer needs the bit, he's not allowed to even approach the bit — he doesn't even get a temporary reward by touching it. Then I let him go until he tries to take charge, right away I take it back and teach him it's not his bit. Anybody who thinks that a true extension is done by making the horse go more strongly into the bridle by pulling on the reins is foolish. It is true that the reins become more like sticks, but that's because as the horse goes more forward and more through, the neck fills up. It stretches toward the bit. The whole horse steps toward it and your reins become stretched, but not pulling out of your hands. If you like to ride with a horse who is very, very strong on the bit, then you have to have a back and a leg to match.

Carol Lavell

My horse switches leads behind and canters disunited almost every time I try to collect him from the medium or extended canter. What do I do?

I would ride down the long side into the corner at the extended canter. I would keep pushing with my inside leg, keeping my inside hand steady and being careful on the outside rein. Usually they switch leads when they get into a corner, because they don't want to put more weight on their quarters so it's easier to switch. I just keep pushing until they switch back so that they realize it doesn't help them. If they keep being asked to go forward and stay balanced, they actually find it's easier to be on the correct lead.

Bent Jensen

I would use more outside rein. I also, as an exercise, might come to the collection and make a ten-meter circle to the inside to produce the stretching of the outside and the bending of the inside. Every time I would feel that coming I'd try to bring the shoulders fore and ride a ten-meter circle.

Carol Grant Oldford

Is there a prerequisite for introducing counter-canter? How do you know when your horse is ready?

I have found the counter-canter to be easy with every horse that I've ever trained. What I observe is that as soon as the horse is in counter-canter, the rider immediately stiffens against the horse's movement, even on a straight line. Starting the counter-canter, you have not only to begin with the easiest possible huge turns but your geometry has to be good so that at no point do you demand a sharper turn that will cause the horse to lose his balance. You have to have a plan for your figures. In the middle levels where we have tests with serpentines in counter-canter, I see riders stiffen and cease allowing the horse to go forward as soon as they start the counter-canter. The horse feels more conflict from the rider then he does in the true canter.

Gary Rockwell

I usually introduce the counter-canter when they're able to balance themselves on a 15-meter circle in the canter. The counter-canter will also improve the balance. I use the counter-canter for horses that tend to be crooked. I have one student who has a horse that was a little bit four-beat in the canter, and it has helped her to find the canter rhythm and find the straightness in canter. We usually start just by going across the diagonal and through the short side in the counter-canter and when the horse and the rider can hold that, then we try to make it all the way around the arena. Once they can hold the counter-canter all the way around the arena, we try to do a 20-meter circle in counter-canter. Then, when they can hold that, we graduate to the serpentine.

Ann Guptill

I introduce counter-canter when I feel the young horse, regardless of whether he is a Training Level horse or a Third Level horse, has achieved a very, very high degree of balance and harmony on the true leads. As I feel him able to do transitions from canter to trot to canter easily, then I might start to go out on the left lead, for instance, towards X and then just allow him to counter-canter back towards the wall — so a very shallow line. After that, with each month, I might add a little more angle to that line until finally I'm able to do a serpentine of three loops that are the width of the arena retaining the counter-canter. When I feel that that's easy for the horse, I might make it more difficult to four loops, finally to six loops and using counter-canters around the short side as well to make sure that the horse always knows that he's to stay straight underneath me, fluid in his canter, and on my aids whether or not I'm on the true lead or the counter lead.

Robert Dover

I start to do it as soon as their canter is balanced enough to do it fairly well. I'll often start coming out of a corner and then just go in towards the center line and then back out to the rail so the horse doesn't have to do it for very long. Then I just make it more and more difficult as they learn to do it.

Charlotte Bredahl

I introduce it fairly early on — maybe with the First Level horse in a very gentle, very systematic way. I might have a rider do a shallow loop down the long side starting at the corner letter, barely coming out to the quarter line when they're across from B or E and back to the corner letter again. And then progressively, as the horse gets stronger and understands, that shallow loop can go out to X. And then you can go across the diagonal and do the short side in counter-canter. Eventually you can ride a full 20-meter circle or serpentine staying on the same lead. But it gets introduced as no big deal with the shallow loop. So, in that case, it can be introduced fairly early. I think what the rider has to keep in mind is that the counter-canter is a collecting exercise and that in order for a horse to be collected, he has to be straight. A lot of the trouble that people get into in counter-canter is once again that they bend the neck of the horse too much. As a result the horse falls on the opposite shoulder and therefore, it's an on-the-forehand exercise rather than a collecting exercise. So I do something kind of unorthodox in that I allow my riders to counter-flex the horse in counter-canter for the same reason that I had them counter-flex them when they were learning the feeling of a straight horse. When you counter-flex the horse in counter-canter (i.e. if you're on the left lead the horse is positioned at the poll to the right) the shoulders will slide back in front of the hindquarters, the body will be straight, allowing the horse to achieve whatever degree of collection your figure is asking for. And once again, the rider learns the feeling of the straight horse in counter-canter. When that's a familiar feeling and everything else feels awkward, then I allow them to flex the horse in the direction of the lead again. But I do a lot of counter-flexing like that in counter-canter, because the horse must be straight. Otherwise the horse is not collected and what's the point of doing counter-canter?

Jane Savoie

What has helped a lot of my Second and Third Level riders is using shoulder-fore in counter-canter, because very often it will help the horse to hold themselves better in counter-canter, and the rider can get a better feel of it using counter-canter and serpentines. An important concept that a lot of riders have trouble with now is the straightness on a serpentine — keeping the horse's body straight while riding a bending line.

Ann Guptill

What are some of the exercises you use for working on a horse's canter?

Canter takes a lot longer than trot to make quality. I refuse to buy a horse with a bad canter ever again. There are a lot of exercises to produce and maintain suppleness in the canter. For the horse who's against one rein, haunches-in into that rein on a straight line. On the left lead canter bend to the left, as much contact on the right rein as you can take, but flex to the hard rein and put the haunches into the rein. This is done on three tracks — only. The shoulders and front legs must travel along a straight line — no wobbling or crossing of the legs. The neck must come squarely out between the shoulder blades. In general, for a young horse training First and Second Level, haunches-in is often too difficult to do because the horse cannot bring the haunches toward the inside rein like that, unless he throws the shoulder out. The rider ends up bringing the haunches further to the left, past the left rein, and the exercise doesn't work. The other exercise is to track to the right after you've done a lot of haunches-in left. Right lead canter with position left, and the haunches up against the wall.

Another exercise for a horse that is against, say, the inside right rein, is to go in right lead canter. The rider's inside leg places the right hind leg to the left. Don't pull on the right rein at all. Let go of the right rein.

Supple the horse from the left rein and take the right hind leg and put it toward the left jaw and stay on the circle to the right. Do lots of bigger canter, smaller canter on a big circle that way. And then you'd be surprised coming around back to the right, suppling the horse will be better on the right because the right hind leg takes more of the weight of the body. You've given up pulling on the inside rein, the direct effect of which is to interfere with the work of the right hind leg.

Carol Lavell

My horse is very heavy and resistant on the inside rein at the canter. What can I do to fix this?

A lot of the resistance to the inside rein can be because the horse has such a big canter, and that inside hind leg comes swinging forward, and he just can't give to the inside. So he has to push against the bit. That's so obvious in Warmbloods with big canters. They can't give it. I don't generally let my riders touch the inside rein when they develop the canter on horses with a big canter. They don't have any bend at all to the inside and that's fine with me. Then, as long as they don't touch that inside rein and learn to use the outside rein, the horse learns to use his inside hind leg to balance himself out and he doesn't get resistant. He may start really tough, but the riders I see really fighting with that inside rein, trying to get it from them, bending the horse to the inside, keeping him on a circle and constantly bending the neck to the inside, have minimal results. They don't get the rein from the horse, and the horse learns to be more frantic and more resistant.

We also use leg-yield in canter. I'm on the right lead on a straight line and I leg yield from my right lead and push the horse toward the left rein. And I don't try to bend the horse's neck. I try to keep him straight and just push him off to the left until he starts falling to the left. Then, on the right lead on a straight line, I push the horse to the left from my right leg and I position and flex a little bit left and right and he becomes a little more supple, more capable of moving his balancing poles — head and neck, and still standing on his own legs. And I do it to both sides. When I say leg yield at canter, many times the people are on one lead or anther and they say, "which way?" and I say I really don't care. I don't care if they go toward the right lead in leg yield and flex the horse left and right, or they move away from the right lead. It's a good exercise to make the horse bend his joints and make him more mobile and not fixed in a straight line. Part of making the horse straight is to make him manipulable and part of making a good canter is to make the joints bend and make the horse's body moveable in the canter. You can't fix a canter without moving the parts. Finally, the most valuable canter exercise for me with upper level horses is shoulder-in staying on the center line. The center line is the focus of the most difficult canter exercises in Grand Prix and staying straight and balanced on it is a real test of your ability. Just as long as the rider remembers that all exercises can be tools like double edged swords. There are advantages and disadvantages in each exercise. Remember to be aware of both!

Carol Lavell

What are some of the most common faults you see at counter-canter?

The horse has to be balanced. The rider has to consider that regardless of the direction they're going they are still riding left or right canter. The common faults I see are people either overbending to the outside to try and oversupport the counter-canter, consequently throwing the horse in onto their inside shoulder and upsetting his balance, or bending the horse in the opposite direction — to the inside of the circle when they're on the counter lead, the result being that the horse slides his hindquarters out around the circle and again loses his balance. The primary concern is to make sure that the horse and rider are balanced.

Belinda Nairn

The balance has to be there, engagement. The horse has to remain supple. He has to be ridden very well off the outside rein. In the beginning, the young horse might not accept the outside rein well enough and he might curl his body too much and then riders try to correct too much with the inside reins when indeed they have to be able to go in straight lines through the outside rein and produce the same thing we have to produce in all gaits — what we call relative straightness on the outside.

Carol Grant Oldford

Every time I put my horse in counter-canter and try to keep it going around the short side, she either changes leads or worse, canters disunited just before we reach the end of the diagonal.

This can be because they're out behind, wide behind, or confused. They need to be ridden forward. The rider needs to keep the canter aid on as they make the turn to counter-canter. Strong outside leg, supporting outside hand and hold the bend to the lead to help the horse maintain the lead.

Ann Guptill

What are some of the common faults in canter half-pass?

The haunches leading is very common. The horse breaks in the middle, the bend is incorrect and they lose the rhythm, falling on their shoulders and forehand. Next would be a horse that's a bit lazy in the canter and the lateral work and they lug on the rider's hands and get down on their forehand and out behind the motion in the canter. The body may be in line, shoulders in front of the hindquarters, shoulders slightly leading in the half-pass, but the horse gets strong in the hands, down on the forehand and four beating behind because they get heavy in front and light behind. Another common fault is horses that curl up. The solution is to go forward. To help prevent these faults, the horse should be schooled forward in shoulder-fore in all preparations for half-pass work.

Ann Guptill

CHAPTER 8

Lateral Movements

My students often seem to have a block about learning to ride shoulder-in. Maybe I'm not explaining it in a way they can understand. Do you have any advice?

A lot of times what I see in the very beginning with people doing a shoulder-in is that they pull the horse's head and think they're riding a shoulder-in, but actually it's nothing at all. As I try to describe it to them, the horse is about 30 degrees off the wall, and the movement is on three tracks. I tell them that if the horse were to be dragging his toes in the dirt he would leave three lines — his outer hind leg is on the outside line, the inside hind leg and outside front leg are on the middle line, and the inside front leg is on the inside line. I try to get the rider to match his right hand with the horse's right front leg and his left hip with the horse's left hind for doing a left shoulder-in. I tell them to try to keep that line parallel to the wall. That's something that they can actually feel when they're riding. Make them look down and see if that fist is on that middle line. The horse must also keep his hind legs from crossing so the rider must use their outer leg.

Gwen Blake

Can you offer any tips for teaching a horse to do shoulder-in?

Most of the problems stem from bad rider position, I think, and so I always try to work on the rider's position first and, of course, he must be able to leg-yield before he can do a shoulder-in. Some people start a shoulder-in and the horse just goes to the middle of the ring so they must make sure that they know how to at least use their legs. But I like to imagine that the rider's legs belong to the horse's hind legs and the front end of their body, from the belt up, belongs to the front end of the horse. So the rider's hips must stay going straight but her front end must bring the horse's shoulders off the track. So they don't bring their outside hip forward, but their hand has to go forward a little bit.

Carol Grant Oldford

How does the concept of straightness carry into shoulder-in?

The classical way says you cannot execute a proper shoulder-in and should not be practicing a shoulder-in until the horse is collected. Yet shoulder-in is a collecting exercise, if it's done properly, and it's the world's finest collecting exercise for sure. Unfortunately, hardly anybody can do it right, because they don't understand the aids: the horse has to be between the inside leg and the outside rein, and he has to step toward the inside rein, not be pulled in and bent with the inside rein and all the feet stepping away from it to the outside. What I see nearly 100% of the time in the United States is: pull on the inside rein, push the horse with the inside leg to the outside rein, and he steps away going over the shoulder to the outside with the inside hip to the outside and the outside hip and hind leg dragging behind the horse. People who are doing this have absolutely no idea about straightness in a horse. Straightness here means that you ride both hind legs up under the shoulders and the horse steps up to the inside rein — he's not pulled around with it. And he supples and gives to it, and you can ride between the reins in shoulder-in, neck coming out between the shoulders. This takes years to do right — not just the first few months of Second Level. And one side will always be defective.

Carol Lavell

I keep hearing that I could be using more lateral movements to improve my horse's canter. Do you have any suggestions as to which movements would be most helpful?

Using shoulder-fore, we school turns onto the centerline to hold the balance on the centerline, because at Third and Fourth Level they have to enter in canter, and they have to halt on the centerline. Also, canter half-passes come from the centerline so we school the centerline in shoulder-fore.

I don't very often use the travers or the haunches-in for this turn unless the horse is very stiff on that side or is having difficulty with one hind leg not stepping under enough. I use the haunches-in if they're very stiff on one side or having trouble with one particular hind leg. I will also use haunches-in when beginning to do schooling pirouettes. We then do small circles in haunches-in in the canter to teach the horse to balance in the pirouette and to help develop the strength of the hindquarters to perform a pirouette. Most of our canter work is done in shoulder-fore including the counter-canter. I also use shoulder-fore in schooling lengthenings and medium gaits to keep straightness and on the diagonal when schooling the flying changes.

Ann Guptill

How do I know when my horse is ready to start half-pass?

I always start the green horse from a ten-meter circle, because he will already have the correct bend for half-pass. I like to do this in the corner, so that I leave a ten-meter half circle on the centerline and then go back to the track. This is easier for the green horse. Another consideration is that the horse will do better half-passes from the gait in which he has more talent and suppleness.

Bent Jensen

In half-pass, a horse has made a clear departure from leg yielding exercises, which can allow the horse to be slightly on the forehand. Before beginning half-pass the horse should be able to perform a good shoulder-in and travers. In half-pass, the horse must place his weight to the hind end, so you know he is ready for half-pass, because he has the strength to do this.

I train it usually in the walk, before training it in the trot to give the horse the sense and pattern of half-pass. I start with a ten-meter circle, from the centerline, then go to shoulder-in for a few steps then to half-pass. If the horse loses the bend or begins to lean on his inside shoulder or inside rein then I make a volte in walk and ride shoulder-in again. When he is accepting the inside leg correctly, then I continue to half-pass. I repeat it until he understands, and then I ride it in the trot. As he progresses in strength and understanding, he is able to maintain a relaxed back, keep his hind legs engaged, and maintain the correct bend and angle.

Half-pass is travers on the diagonal line. I find in teaching this concept, that it seems to help riders to de-emphasize the tendency to over use the inside rein in half-pass. Overuse of the inside rein can cause a horse to lean on the inside shoulder in self-defense, become heavy on that rein and subsequently to lose the bend.

Kathy Connelly

I train it as soon as he learns haunches-in. As soon as he can keep the rhythm the same and he's able to stay strong and is very confirmed. Of course, he's at least confirmed in the shoulder-in before I teach the haunches-in and so both those movements are confirmed before I attempt the half-pass. I then take him into the same haunches-in on a line that doesn't have the support of the wall, for example, the quarterline or the centerline. And I teach the half-pass out from the corner, starting like a shoulder-fore, I'm getting the horse pushed into the outer rein. I teach it as if it's haunches-in on diagonal line. A lot of times what happens with a green horse, again due to lack of strength, is that he tries to escape that movement. When I feel that happens where he loses his balance, I take him at that point and I push him on to a straight line, for example, the quarterline, and push him directly into a shoulder-in. Once he's balanced again at that then I attempt again a few more steps with the horse thinking he's doing haunches-in on a diagonal line, and I continue on until he can take the whole diagonal.

Gwen Blake

Half-pass is my downfall. My horse never really feels engaged. Instead he just feels like he's falling sideways. What am I doing wrong?

Very commonly the rider sits to the outside trying to put their weight into the outer leg instead of using their inner leg to drive the horse's hind leg under to the outside rein. The other thing I see a lot are riders pushing the haunches way ahead thinking that there needs to be more bend and they get the wrong type of bend which causes the horse to pull himself over, weakening himself rather than pushing with the hindquarters. That is where they lose their idea of shoulder-in. They just want to get the horse's hindquarters over. Another thing I see a lot is that as soon as the horse gets about a meter away from the wall, the rider continues to ride on straight. The haunches have not completed the half-pass, and it just kind of dwindles away at the end. I try to teach students to finish the half-pass, and I even sometimes throw in an exercise where they get towards the wall to push the horse into renvers down the wall to confirm the idea of finishing or completing the full line.

Gwen Blake

The most common fault is haunches leading. You have to think shoulder-fore a little bit in the beginning and go with the shoulders leading and then pick up the haunches to get into the right angle.

For the more advanced horse, one exercise that I feel really helps the half-pass, especially in the trot, is to change tempo. I go in a big tempo, slow down, half-halt and then go back to the bigger tempo. What I really like is for the inside front leg to reach out. If you're not getting that, you have to ride inside leg, outside rein, but

Carole Grant Oldford riding Tolerant in the extended trot. Photo by Terri Miller.

if the horse needs to be more bent, you have to ride inside leg, inside hand. The greater the bend, the less front leg you get. I decide when to apply either of these techniques, depending on what a particular horse needs at the moment.

Bent Jensen

My horse tends to leave his haunches behind in half-pass. How can I get him more engaged?

An exercise that is very good is starting with shoulder-in to half-pass, and then finishing in renvers. You can begin on the centerline in shoulder-in, then ride to your half-pass. Continue in half-pass until the quarter marker and then ride to renvers, and finish the half-pass with the haunches slightly leading. In this exercise, the horse must work with his back and hind legs more to maintain the engagement. This is a wonderful exercise for horses that tend to trail their haunches at the end of the half-pass. The rider must be aware of the horse's haunches, so that he can control the haunches from leading at times when this exercise is not being intentionally ridden.

Another exercise that is helpful to develop more engagement is counter change in the half-pass. First to ride shoulder-in right proceeding to half pass right.

Then to ride to left shoulder-in proceeding to left half-pass, etc. The rider should remain in shoulder-in until the horse is honest each time to the new inside leg. The horse must not shift weight laterally to either shoulder, but should keep his weight centered. Another helpful exercise in half-pass is to begin on the long side in shoulder-in left, for example, proceed to half-pass left for about eight strides, then proceed in travers left on a straight line for a few strides, then shoulder-in left for a few strides and then resume half-pass left. This exercise contributes to the suppleness of the horse enormously and increases his sensitivity level to the rider's seat and leg aids.

Another exercise for half-pass to increase suppleness and engagement is to ride the horse across the diagonal alternating a few strides of half-pass right, then leg yield a few strides by changing the bend to the left but continuing to move to the right — then change the bend to the right again to resume the half-pass right, etc. Attention must be paid to keeping the horses's center of balance so that he does not fall on his left or right shoulder. There are many other exercises that one can do to increase engagement in the half-pass, these are just a couple of them.

Kathy Connelly

It's so hard to convey correct feel to students. One of my biggest problems is teaching correct half-pass.

A lot of times I find that they're doing it incorrectly, thinking that their main goal is to take the horse sideways and they push from the outer leg to the inner rein and therefore they lean actually to the outside over the wrong seatbone and cause a lot of problems. Again I tell them to think of doing haunches-in on an imaginary diagonal line. I ask them to keep pushing them from haunches-in into shoulder-in encouraging them to feel that it's the exact same aid as for haunches-in and shoulder-in, outer rein.

If the horse starts falling out from underneath them, they have to reconfirm their inner leg to outer rein.

Gwen Blake

CHAPTER 9

Halt and Rein-Back

Q

What are the correct aids for rein back?

Move both legs back a little, sit up straight and ride the horse forward into the bit from a light leg and then close the hands in the half-halt until the horse understands that he comes lightly forward to the bridle, making his steps backwards with diagonal pairs. The horse should never be pulled with the reins if he doesn't back up. That's how most of the problems begin, and that's why I always start horses with someone on the ground to tap his front legs so that he understands the rein-back.

Bent Jensen

Q

I'm having real problems teaching my horse to rein-back correctly without just pulling him back. He either steps sideways behind or just tucks up into a tight little ball and doesn't move.

The rein-back is difficult for the horse to learn, because he can't see where he is going and also because the usual emphasis is on going forward. However, this is true also of rein-back, because the horse has to go forward into the bridle and then rein back. To train rein-back, I always have a person on the ground with a whip to touch the front leg to give the horse the idea.

Bent Jensen

I never seem to get a decent score for rein-back even though my horse backs up perfectly readily. What am I doing wrong?

Some of the common faults are stiffening in the poll, coming above the bit as he reins back, and making short stiff steps. The horse that goes sideways is bringing his haunches to one side or the other rather than going straight. Another fault is the horse that runs backwards rather than taking slow, measured quiet steps. Another problem is the horse that leans on the bit and won't back up, because he's so much on the forehand.

The correction is to ride the correct aids for rein-back repeatedly and to reward the horse when he does it correctly but not to punish him. Most horses learn to rein-back incorrectly because they are taught incorrectly — usually with too much rein rather than a correct interaction of the seat, leg and reins. The proper way to correct this fault is to ride the correct aids and be rewarding. If the horse tends to be crooked, do the rein back with the horse next to the wall so that you can use the wall to train him to be straight.

Bent Jensen

What do you look for as a judge to be characteristics of a good rein-back and how do you train rein-back?

That's a very difficult question because it's probably my greatest nemesis. I think it's a very tricky thing. Important for the judge is that the legs are diagonally paired, and the horse is willing to accept the bridle and doesn't drag his front feet. Sometimes when I'm teaching rein-back, I try to think about reining back the front leg and to make my half-halt so short that I only take the front legs and I never pull further back into the hind legs.

Carol Grant Oldford

As a judge, the characteristics of a good rein-back are that the horse steps backwards with alternate diagonal pairs in a straight line. There should be no sideways deviation of a hind leg and the horse's feet should distinctly leave the ground — no toe dragging.

To train rein-back can be difficult because it is not natural for a horse to go backwards, where he cannot see. So the horse must have confidence in our aids. The horse must be able to shift his center of gravity onto his hind legs in the halt. The horse also needs to understand halt from the walk and the trot. The rider should keep a light seat to encourage the horse to remain relaxed in his back, and the horse should be straight and accepting the bit. The leg of the rider should remain in contact with the horse and as the horse's impulse is to step forward the rider half-halts to encourage a backward step. It never helps to pull and oftentimes makes training rein back difficult or a problem because horses will become defensive in the back, poll and jaw and lean on the bit.

It is helpful to have someone on the ground to assist in training the concept of rein-back to the horse. The ground person can tap the horse on the chest or front legs and cluck as the rider applies the aids for rein-back.

Another technique that I use often in teaching rein-back is that I create a three sided rectangle with jumping rails flat on the ground. Then I walk or trot the horse in and halt. I gently give him the aids for rein-back. I repeat them without pulling harder. It then occurs to the horse to back up because that is the only way out of the three sided rectangle. I repeat this several times with rewards each time. When the horse associates the aids with rein-back — I can then repeat the exercise without having to be in the rectangle. It is an easy way to train rein-back and avoids a lot of confusion.

Kathy Connelly

How do you train a horse to halt squarely from the trot and from the canter?

I think in canter it's something you must practice. You have to go down there and make sure you collect and go forward and collect and go forward. And when you can really do that and the horse accepts you to collect him and send him forward, then you settle softly into a nice halt. And if you allow him early in his training to go down there and clunk down in the halt, he just kind of imitates that for the rest of his life.

In trot, when I ask a horse to trot forward, I make sure that I have a steady position to the inside, an outside rein and outside leg. I don't want to make a counter-bend at that moment of coming to halt. I want to keep my corridor very steady and ride right through it.

Carol Grant Oldford

I rarely achieve immobility in the halt. My horse always fidgets or starts to move off. At one clinic I was told to fix this by making him stand for 20 seconds. This only seems to make the problem worse.

I have a student who has a horse that gets very nervous at the halt and we've managed to keep him very quiet by not asking for a long halt. When coming into the halt, we put our hands down on the withers and give him a little scratch and we find that settles him a little bit. Then we move off. As time goes on, we let his halt become longer and longer. Whereas when we tried to halt him for quite a long time and insist that he stand there, that seemed to make him more upset. So we found if we just halted for a short time, (not come in halt — boom — and go off, that wound him up) let him relax, gave him a little scratch, and made him think he was finished and then go on, he seemed to settle more.

Gwen Blake

CHAPTER 10

Flying Changes and Pirouettes

Q I had always understood that a simple lead change was done by walking or trotting a few steps and then picking up the new lead. Is there a more specific standard?

A balanced simple change shows three strides of walk or trot between each canter lead. Usually you see running and hurrying through the change. Mistakes will be due to a greenness on the horse's part and very often a greenness on the rider's part. If the rider has this problem with the simple changes they should not be too concerned with the number of strides between each canter transition but rather with the balance of the horse between the transitions. And when the horse is quietly on the aids in the transitions, closing up the distance between the transitions will be no problem.

Ann Guptill

Q How can you tell when your horse is ready to do flying changes?

A lot of times the horses offer to do it themselves in the beginning. You do counter-canter and they do a change. I've taught a lot of my horses that way. When they do them, I just reward them. I never punish a horse for changing when they do counter-canter like that at the beginning. So most of my horses have actually learned flying changes before they've learned to hold the counter-canter.

I think that's an easy way to do it, because there's never really a real conflict. I know that was the case with Monsieur when I started him. He could hardly do a 20-meter circle, and he just started doing changes because he thought it was sort of fun and I just rewarded him for it and it didn't take long before they were pretty confirmed.

Charlotte Bredahl

I start by riding a lot of simple changes through the walk and shortening up — riding on the circle with lots of simple changes, counter-canter, simple change, regular canter. And then practicing to make the horse really straight and understanding the use of the new outer rein to make the horse really straight.

Jessica Ransehousen

My prerequisite for flying changes is that they have to be able to do half-passes at canter, not that they have to do them perfectly, but they have to understand the concept and be able to maintain their bend and go forward and sideways in some semblance of balance in both directions. They have to know counter-canter and hold it in a dressage arena — not a big field, but 20 x 40 x or 20 x 60 size arena and they have to be able to do simple transitions, canter-walk-canter. Again not that they're going to get 8's in a competition arena but they have to be able to do it and take up the correct lead regardless of what direction you're going. You should be able to go on the wall and canter left, walk and canter right, and they should be able to do ten-meter circles comfortably. The reason they have to know all that is because: 1) they have to have sufficient balance, 2) they have to be on the aids enough because if they're a little nervous or bully, they'll start doing changes themselves — not on the rider's aids.

Pam Goodrich

Jolicoeur was really a training challenge, because he was incredibly crooked. I would ask for a change and the shoulders would just fly to the outside and the haunches would come in. I had to make a physical barrier for him. Normally, when you ride a change, you half-halt the new outside rein basically by closing your hand in a fist, but I had to do more than that with him. I had to make a physical barrier to his shoulder falling out. Not only did I close my hand in a fist, but also I moved it laterally in the direction of the new lead to hold his shoulder over his new inside hind leg. We really got quite good scores for changes but I always had to ride them with this correction. Zapatero came with super changes, absolutely super changes. What I worked on with him was striving to make the changes more expressive by making them more uphill. Genaldon was fairly simple. What I made sure I had was a good collected canter, a good counter-canter, and good simple changes of lead. Those three things were my foundation. By working on those things you can work on flying changes without even riding one change. You lay a foundation with those things and then the changes are simple to do.

Jane Savoie

It is absolutely necessary that the horse has achieved some collection in his canter first, and that he makes absolutely perfect walk, canter, walk transitions without a flaw. He must be sharp to the aids, because if there is any delay between your asking the horse to canter and when he actually does it, then he's not yet ready to start the flying changes. I like to start the changes at the end of a half-pass, or on the circle from the counter-canter. If the horse is really obedient and sharp to the aids and has a good balance in the canter, then the flying changes are easy.

Gary Rockwell

You have to make sure first that the basic canter and the counter-canter are balanced. I like to school a lot of simple changes through the walk to make sure the horse can do that correctly, coming down to the walk in a frame, keeping the walk clear and then coming back up into the canter, keeping the frame so that we know he is balanced. I like to also make sure the horse can perform a 12-meter counter-canter circle he can be that engaged, and then you just go for it!

The first time I attempt a flying change is from a half-pass to another shallow half-pass or shoulder fore and I usually find that's quite successful and they don't get really nervous, because they're comfortable returning back into a lateral movement that they've schooled several times before.

Gwen Blake

I want to make sure that he accepts the leg well and that he has learned how to do a turn on the forehand. Very early on he must already be able to do a little bit of half-pass, and he must be able to move away from the leg very well so that right away he doesn't learn to kick and be naughty against the leg. And then whenever I prepare a horse for his first flying changes I always set up a bridge for him. For example, a half-pass exercise would be a bridge before the flying change or schooling pirouette might be the bridge to make his wheels all aligned and to supple him so that the change and the engagement and the suppleness are already set up.

Carol Grant Oldford

I think the horse has to be on the aids and he should feel comfortable and balanced in counter-canter before starting flying changes. He should be responsive to your legs, responsive to the half-halts and transitions, particularly walk-canter transitions. If I assume the horse is prepared in this sense, that he's collected and balanced, and responsive to the leg, the way I like to introduce flying changes is on a 20-meter circle. I start by doing a lot of walk-canter-canter-walk transitions and then graduate into canter-walk-counter-canter-walk transitions until that's easy. Some horses will pick this up in five minutes, and some horses may take two or three days or a week to be completely relaxed. Assuming the horse picks it up quickly and is relaxed, I'll go to the next step, which is to pick up the counter-canter, do a flying change and finish it with the walk transition. This way it's the same pattern that the horse has learned, and the flying change fits in as a simple part of the exercise, rather than an unfamiliar new movement which can often seem threatening. With the walk transition following the change, this eliminates any anxiety for a horse that might anticipate or become excited. I don't punish the horse if the changes are late behind or if they make any mistake until they're comfortable in making some sort of flying change. However, once they're comfortable I demand that the horse make a clean flying change. I use the same basic pattern, but demand much more collection. My objective is to get the horse to think about his hindquarters, so I try to get the canter a little bit quicker and shorter than might seem ideal, just to make him sit down and quicken his hind legs. Depending on the horse, I will sometimes tap the horse lightly with the whip at the moment I ask for the change — again to get the horse to focus on his hind legs. As previously, I follow the change with a walk transition to eliminate tension and remember that reward is the essence of training, to encourage the horse to want to try again.

Belinda Nairn

What should one look for in a correct flying change?

You want the flying change to have lots of expression and height in the front. The rhythm, again, should stay the same. You have to change within that same rhythm. Also, the straightness is really important. When you look at a green horse who is first learning his changes, a lot of times he changes very crookedly and again that's due to the horse not quite having the balance and the strength. A more advanced horse has to be straighter, higher in the front, reaching and in rhythm.

Gwen Blake

A good flying change should be as good as the best stride of the normal canter. There has to be a great degree of expression within the change just as there should be within the normal collected canter. Expression means that you have a clear bound over the ground with an engaged hind leg. I like to see some knee action in the front meaning that the horse is lifting his front legs as well as his hind legs over the ground. So, harmony, absolute straightness, and a very expressive stride from one lead to the other.

Robert Dover

What are the most common faults in flying changes?

Horses that are difficult in the flying change are often not very obedient and supple and relaxed in the canter. Usually I find that I have to go back and make them more obedient to the aids in the simple changes and more straight and more relaxed in the canter.

Gary Rockwell

Common faults in the flying changes are horses that change late in front or late behind or get very crooked in the change. Of all these faults, late behind is the worst. In a green horse it's okay if he comes above the bit a little bit in the change, but the change has to be clean behind. If a horse learns how to change late behind, it's very difficult to ride that out of them.

Ann Guptill

My horse changes easily in one direction, but he's extremely difficult and stiff on the other side. Is there any way to work on this?

Horses tend to have a difficult side. I'll go from the correct lead to counter-canter on the hard change and again I use the whip in the change — just a touch with the whip at the same time I ask and that usually gets the hind leg to come under better.

Charlotte Bredahl

I'm one of those people who says go ahead and do it from the one direction for a while first until they're sure. I think that's easier rather than being really heroic and trying to get it the hard way first.

Jessica Ransehousen

Usually this is because that lead itself is not as comfortable for him, so he would rather not go to it. This means that I would look for the problem and its root and I would try to make that lead more comfortable, better balanced, through the use of all the exercises up to that. Once I knew that that lead was just as good as the other lead, I would go back and try to perfect the flying change to that lead again. And usually when the horse is comfortable on both leads in an equal way, his flying changes will also be equal in both directions.

Robert Dover

My horse is almost always late behind in his changes. Why is this and what do I do?

The timing of the rider is very important. It's very important in teaching flying changes that there be two people. An experienced person should be on the horse's back with an experienced person with a good eye on the ground who can recognize any mistakes. Very often a young horse will try to rush through the change. If the horse is tense in the back, the rider may not be able to feel what the hind legs are doing in the change. You might ask for a little bit of haunches-in to help the horse. Using haunches-in or a large schooling pirouette will help the rider teach the horse to use both hind legs equally and engage more behind for a better change.

Ann Guptill

That's difficult, because it depends upon why it's happening. It might be that being late behind is because the horse slows down in the canter when it's time to make a change instead of being able to drive a little bit more accurately off the hind legs.

Jessica Ransehousen

I go back to asking the horse to carry himself in a collected canter and I try to strengthen him by giving him exercises to bring him back on his hindquarters and yet speed up the hindquarters without taking the whole horse back so that he has to use his hindquarters and his back to carry his weight. I call this putting the horse on the spot. I do several of those exercises to get him comfortable and confident that he's able to carry himself and that will get rid of this problem.

Gwen Blake

There are a couple of exercises geared to physically help the horse do a good change. You can mentally prepare him for not changing late behind by putting his mind into his new outside hind leg which is the strike-off leg. A lot of times what I'll have the rider do is carry the whip in the inside hand and count to three while giving three light taps with the whip — one, two, three — so that they put the horse's attention into that hind leg. Do this several times and then finally one, two, three, change. In this way the horse's mind is on the hind leg that you want him to strike off with. With regard to horses that change late in front, for the most part I find it comes from restriction from the rider. The rider needs to soften the new inside hand forward at the moment he gives the aids to change.

Two of my favorite exercises for that are to: 1. increase the degree of collection prior to the change. The most "collected" thing I can think of doing in the canter is the pirouette. So I'll do a schooling pirouette and really get the horse sitting and carrying weight behind. Then I leave the pirouette and immediately ask for the change. 2. With a lot of horses that don't change clean, I find that there is a lack of throughness on the new inside of their body. If I can put them through that side of their body, then they don't feel a barrier — a blockage — to jumping through with the new inside hind. So once again I go back to my sort of unusual method of bending the horse away from the lead. I had a horse that I rode once many years ago who had been changing late behind for at least a year. I spent six weeks with him not doing a single change. Instead I went all the way around the arena doing this exercise (i.e. riding left lead canter with him bent to the right). I did this during true canter, counter-canter, serpentines, and circles until he was very soft on the outside of his body, which was going to become the new inside of his body. Six weeks later when I finally straightened him and asked for a change, it was clean. So, I hate to use unorthodox things per se because we talk about classical training, but when you are dealing with a problem horse, if it works, do it. You have to find some way to put their bodies in a position so that they can learn to use themselves in a different way.

Jane Savoie

Many times I find that it works better to do some correct canter to counter-canter on the long side. I usually find with the horse who likes to be late, that if you take a really good half-halt on what's going to be the new outside rein, and sometimes use the whip also on the outside all at the same time as you give the aids with your legs that that works really well. And of course you release some of the inside rein. Most of the time you see that people are not releasing on the new inside rein — at least I see that all the time when I teach — that people hang onto the new inside rein and then the horse cannot come through behind and I think a lot of horses are late for that reason when they're started that way.

Charlotte Bredahl

The horse that changes late has to be dealt with very, very quickly. Usually if he's changing late behind, it is coming from either an inaccuracy in the way the rider is asking for the flying change, or the horse is not thoroughly engaged and in perfect balance in his canter. If the canter is sufficiently engaged and properly balanced but the horse still doesn't understand how to change with the hind leg leading, then what you want to do is imagine that each flying change will only change behind when you ask and to try to prevent the horse from even changing in front at all. Usually this will produce a successful flying change, and the horse, having learned how to do the flying change will realize that it's much more comfortable to do it that way than to change late behind and then have to deal with it a stride later.

Robert Dover

That's a problem I seldom have when the horse is good on the leg. When he's in front of the leg and I set up the bridge, I don't have the late behind problem. I do have it late in front many times in the beginning and that's because they're blocked in the hand and haven't come all the way through. If I were to get a horse and the problems were there, of course I'd have to go back to the basics and I'd have to teach them to be better on the leg and maybe come over their back a little bit better and be able to be more elastic.

Carol Grant Oldford

How do you work with horses who change late in front?

Changing late in front usually has to do with the animal's not being able to sufficiently balance his forehand while it's in the air and so he leaves his forehand too earthbound the second of the change. Since he doesn't have the opening for his inner front leg to change with his outer front leg in the air, he leaves himself on the wrong lead still in front as he changes behind. The thing to do about that is to make sure that the horse has his hind legs sufficiently underneath him so that his front end has mobility in the air. And then the proper half-halt of the outside rein, while giving the inner rein, allows the horse to jump with his front end in such a way that he can bring his inner foreleg forward to be that last beat.

Robert Dover

What are the prerequisites for starting tempi changes?

Once the horse is comfortable and relaxed in the single flying changes, then I begin the tempi changes. I usually use the short diagonal, i.e. K to B, or M to E.

On the long diagonal, there is more room to drift and get in trouble. When you come onto the short diagonal from the corner, the horse is really well connected on the outside rein, and it is easier to maintain straightness. Perhaps I will just do two or three changes — the number does not matter — I wait until they are ready. The idea is to teach the concept of sequence — no big deal, without too much excitement. I always wait until they are straight before doing the next change. In each session, I do lines with no changes in the middle of the session, and at the end of the session so that they also learn, at the beginning, that they wait for the request. Then I go to the long diagonal or the quarter marker line once the horse has learned to relax in the tempis. It helps to school pirouettes before practicing the tempi changes, because the quality of the canter is better because of the increased collection, thereby making it easier to keep the horse straight.

Kathy Connelly

To teach the horse you start out with two first and then three and if he's doing the two's very well and the one's are still not good on your leg, then I make the two's much quicker, must faster until I come to the one's. But I might do one or two lines of the two's very quick, very fast and very ahead of my leg and then the one's when I start them should be easier. For the rider it's much harder to learn the one's and really he must be on an experienced horse to learn it.

Carol Grant Oldford

I can't seem to keep my horse's body straight when doing tempi changes. Do you have any advice?

If the horse wants to be crooked, I do the changes on the rail a lot — close to the rail especially if you're inside and you have a wall, I ride them really close to the wall when I practice especially tempi changes to keep them straight. When I try these changes at home I almost always do them on the rail rather than on the diagonal, because it really helps them to keep straight and to learn to always do them straight. And very forward.

Charlotte Bredahl

Once he learns and confirms the flying change, then you have to start working on your straightness. A lot of times a horse changes crookedly because of weakness and being a little bit unsure of what he is doing. A lot of times you can tell him and do your change along the fence line and give him some sort of line to change on to help balance him. Many people tend to do a flying change in the same place which often leads to anticipation in the horse, resulting in crookedness. Attempt the changes in different places, perhaps even from counter-canter to counter-canter.

Gwen Blake

That's where that new inner bending — you know the new inner rein — making the horse really straight to the new inner rein helps a lot first and then ask him with the outside rein and outside leg.

Jessica Ransehousen

I school the diagonals in shoulder-fore, on the outside aids. Come across the diagonal. If the horse drifts after the change, half-halt, shoulder-fore, until the outside aids keep the horse straight in the change.

Ann Guptill

In the upper levels you have the problem of crookedness in flying changes, crookedness that the horse makes when he's in the air, and not just the crookedness when he's on the ground. It is in the air you cannot correct the crookedness. The horse is in the air and he cannot respond. It's even more difficult to correct. It goes back to the basic work where the horse is made even on both sides before you do the flying changes. When you're teaching the flying changes, he will be crooked to one side, for sure. For example, I have a horse who is crooked with the shoulders left and the hips right and I do all my right flying changes with his head to the left not looking to the right. And I start him off with his hips left and his neck left and I do the flying change to the right. Then of course he wants to take a dive to the right as fast as he can go or fall on the right leg and I just have to use more right leg and it's a progressive thing. Trainers must understand that you have to play with these things. You may have a horse who is not collected and he tries constantly to fall off the line, he may be straight in his body but the crookedness shows when you do flying changes and he loses his balance and falls off the line to the right or left even though he's straight in his body and the changes are straight — not swinging the hip, not throwing the shoulders around. A good exercise is if he falls to the right, for example, is to make a 15-meter circle to the left and do the flying change to the right to the outside of the circle. Make the changes in quick succession so he has to get more and more bounce and his quarters stay underneath him on the circle. That's an extremely difficult exercise, but extremely effective in balancing, engaging and straightening an upper level horse. He doesn't have time to make a flying change to the outside fall out and get back to the inside change on time. And when you won't let him fall to the outside, he tries to be late in the change or not make the change at all and you let him make the mistake, and you just keep pushing the hind legs until he can do it. It works right away. It doesn't take weeks and months. It works immediately to correct the crookedness. In order to correct in a very cadenced movement in upper levels, you end up by frequently turning the hips and shoulder even in the trot, even in the passage, and piaffe in order to get the hind legs working more evenly, to move the shoulders in front of the quarters, which is a standard way to correct crookedness. You don't move the quarters to the shoulders, you move the shoulders to the quarters always as a rule. If your horse puts his hips in all the time to make a right lead canter depart, move the shoulders more to the right not the hips to the left.

Carol Lavell

My horse drifts to the right when we are doing tempi changes across the diagonal. By the time we're partway across the diagonal, we're already at B or E.

There are a lot of things that you can do about this: 1) You can concentrate harder on making an imaginary wall next to you. You can also use the actual wall of the arena or the long side of the arena and put the wall next to the horse so that he cannot drift. The more he feels himself being straight and the rider has an opportunity to ride with less severity with his aids, the more the horse will have the initiative to stay straight. So when you're going on a diagonal, for instance, from the right lead, concentrate on keeping a slight flexion to the right as you come out of the corner so that the horse doesn't drift into your right hand and into your right leg. Then straightening, half-halt with right rein to go to the left lead as your right leg comes behind the girth, left leg on the girth, and then if you go back to the right lead it's very important that the right leg be maintained near the girth as the horse jumps into the right lead so that he doesn't jump away from the left leg and then drift to the right.

Robert Dover

Tempi-changes seem such a big step up from single flying changes. How do I know when my horse is ready?

Pretty much as soon as they can do a nice clean change without getting upset about it. When they feel really good, I do another change, but I don't worry about counting at all. I always wait until he's ready for the next change if it's every two or every five or every five and every two — whatever. But I always make sure the horse feels really right in my hand, and I listen to him before I do the next change. I never just say okay now I'm going to do four's which I see a lot even if the horse is totally off the bit. They just keep on going.

Charlotte Bredahl

When the horse is relaxed doing single flying changes, when I do serpentines with changes and changes on straight lines, and the horse is comfortable with that, I go ahead and start tempi changes. And I usually don't wait. I don't spend months on this. I think if they learn changes in a way that is simple to understand, then tempi changes come pretty quickly.

Belinda Nairn

I think the horse has to be balanced and straight in the changes. There should be no tension within the change itself and he should feel confident. In my experience, horses that will do two tempi changes and stay relaxed about it will generally do ones and it won't be a big issue. In starting the one tempis I usually start down the long side staying off the track, and just try to do two ones, changing them out and changing them back, until they'll do that easily in both directions. Sometimes with a sensitive horse I'll go back to the beginning stages and do two ones and walk again, and then pick up the opposite canter and do two ones and walk; so again there's no tendency for the horse to want to rush or lose the collection. When this is easy I'll do two ones, continue to canter a few strides, and then do two more, and gradually add on a change or two as the horse accepts the exercise.

Belinda Nairn

All of the basics as well as a marked degree of collection. I feel that to do the one tempis the horse has to have a greater degree of collection than he needs to do the fours, three, twos. So if you're doing Fourth Level tempi changes you probably don't have the balance you need to do the ones. You want the horse forward and straight, but you need that greater degree of collection to do the one tempis.

Jane Savoie

I introduce them when they can do two tempis comfortably, although not perfectly as they would in a test. I wait until I can do seven or nine two-tempis in good balance, because the biggest problem that horses have in one-tempis is the ability to jump, stride for stride in the same balance. They do one of two things — they either get littler and littler because they don't have enough power behind, or, they're so powerful behind that they get so big they can't do the next change. None of that is the horse's fault. That has to do with their strength and confidence and ability. Therefore, it's not really fair to ask them to do one-tempis if they can't do two-tempis. Once I feel that they can do two-tempis comfortably, I usually will do two one-tempis, just go from one canter lead to the other, and then if they do that pretty well, I'll do three. That will give me an indication of how they'll do the ones. Usually, to evade, they either run away from them or they do them in little tiny strides or they get really crooked. I go back to two-tempis to fix these. If they have the tendency to get little I try doing medium canter two-tempis. If they have the tendency to get too big I try to do little two-tempis. If they end to be very crooked I do them on the wall. And then I go back and I'll do the three and if it's better, then I add two more. If I can get five then the horse knows them and I don't necessarily push for more if I don't think that the horse can hold it. I put them on the back burner for anther two months and usually I can go out and do seven, ten, nine, 15 a couple months later.

Pam Goodrich

Obviously, they have to be solid in the twos. You need to be able to do two-tempis anywhere on the diagonal, on the centerline, or on the wall and quietly everywhere. To do the ones, start across the diagonal and do a couple of twos and then one, one. Again you need that person on the ground, with a good eye who is quick. When they can do one one-tempi each direction then ask three off of each diagonal and leave it. When they can do it, I don't do it every day. Once a week, I will do three ones, and then five ones, and then seven, and then nine. Usually by the time they can do nine ones they understand the concept of one time changes.

Ann Guptill

I always start doing two single ones. And I do that for quite a while until they're really confirmed because usually that doesn't upset them at all. Then you try to do three and you don't try to do more. I think a lot of people get greedy too fast. Then I start moving the one ones closer and closer together rather than doing four or five, I do one, two and then I wait maybe about five steps and I do one, two again. But then as they get better I move them closer together.

Charlotte Bredahl

What do you do to help the horse make the transition from the twos and three to the ones?

One tempi should be as easy as twos and threes. In training the horse to do

Jessica Ransehousen riding Orpheus in the extended trot in the Olympics.
Photo by Jop Kramer.

ones you do not want to produce a scenario where the horse feels that you're being adversarial with him. If I have a horse that is very, very easy to train down to the two tempis, I'll nonchalantly go down the long side in two tempis and then if I'm on the left lead finally I'll just, closing my new outside rein, which would be the left hand, bring my left leg behind the girth, my right leg near the girth. I would ride the flying change out to the counter lead, and then closing my right hand back as he hits the right lead, bring my right leg back a little behind the girth again, my left leg near the girth, I would ask him to change back inwards. So I would get him comfortable at going out and back in, then I might go forward and do a flying change at A and do the same work from counter-canter to true lead and back to counter-canter. Then when I felt that, I would stay on counter-canter, I would do flying change to the true lead back to the counter-canter lead and back to the true lead. Once I knew I had three and they were absolutely straight, then I would feel comfortable possibly the next day to ask for four and then five. Never worry if the horse looks confused from this or if you have a day when suddenly, after you've gotten four ones, the horse becomes unaware that he can even do a single flying change. Relax with that. Take the horse on a hack for a few minutes. Bring him back and try again. You can even take the horse back to the stable, put him away and bring him back out the next day and start over again. What you do look for finally in the one-tempis is that the horse is absolutely straight, expressive, gaining good ground and that there is a look of balance and ease that makes the people that are on the ground have a lot of confidence and enjoy watching it.

Robert Dover

My horse seems to get very overexcited by tempi changes. When we're schooling he gets so quick and silly that I can't imagine showing him. How can I get him past this?

The young horse who is learning will often want to speed up and run. One thing is not to feel desperate about it. What you want to do is make the changes less of a big deal to the horse. If your horse understands four-tempis but wants to run away on the diagonal or on the long side, keep doing four-tempis, even around a large field or around the short side, and every time the horse achieves the next flying change, reward him with your voice. Once the horse has done that change relax again and get the next change. Ride your half-halt, don't override the aids for the flying change, and just make it a very, very nonchalant endeavor. The more you stay relaxed, the more the horse will just realize that he has the opportunity to relax and yet still achieve the goal of getting the tempi changes.

Robert Dover

I do probably what everybody does and that's just make hundreds of changes straight ahead right up against the wall and just keep going and going and going and going and let them be as fussy and silly as they want until they get tired and they start settling down.

Jessica Ransehousen

I periodically go back and make simple changes and single changes relaxed and obedient first. I try making two or three changes and exaggerating the reward. I might start across the diagonal, make two flying changes every six strides and then make a circle there and just try to work the whole thing into the line of succession that's not such a big deal to the horse. I pat the horse on the neck and reward him with my voice when I can to try and keep everything quiet and relaxed.

Gary Rockwell

This can be a difficult problem, because it's done a bit out of nerves where drifting in the changes might be done just a little bit out of laziness or cleverness. Nerves are harder to deal with. Again the horse has to accept the rider's aids. What you need to do is back down to something that uses the same principles but is easier.

If you have trouble with the one-tempis, I back down to four-tempis. If you have trouble with him running, say even in four-tempis, just go across the diagonal, do a flying change, half-halt, get them to accept all the aids again, get the rhythm back then another flying change until you can start closing the distance between the changes. Also using simple changes through the walk to get the back on the aids. Most important in the tempis is to be able to use the aids in between the changes.

Ann Guptill

I don't do tempi changes — I do what's called random changes. What I do is I canter and I do a flying change and then I organize the canter. And I take however long it takes to organize the canter and then I prepare them for the next change and I do that change. I try to get five-tempis, to begin with, so I have five strides to be able to half-halt, meaning rebalance and straighten the horse for the new change, meaning get his shoulders out of the way.

Pam Goodrich

I always think that running is due to a lack of engagement, and so I try to make sure that I just keep sending him forward. If he runs again I'd put him into a bridge, I'd put him into circle work, half-pass work — something to get his running into an active form.

Carol Grant Oldford

Q I find that my horse does his best changes at the beginning of a schooling session and that as we go on he gets more tense and quicker and unbalanced. Why does this happen and how can I work on it?

I think that tempi changes degenerate because the rider loses the collection as each change is done. An exercise that I would do for that is not to count strides but to do a change and then have the horse canter on the spot for three strides as if he's going to go into a pirouette. Then do another change and canter on the spot for three strides so that the horse learns to answer what will eventually become one little half-halt rather than three strides on the spot. In this way the balance can be maintained and it doesn't degenerate as you go across the diagonal line. But for tense horses, for horses that worry, one of the things that is a real pacifier in any exercise is simply repetition until it's not a big deal anymore. In that case I wouldn't want to be interrupted at the end of a diagonal. I would probably go around the outside of the arena or go out into a field and just keep going and going until it's not a big deal. You can also intersperse the changes with something that is relaxing for the horse — something that the horse associates with relaxation of his body. There's any number of things that you can do. You can do a change, and then put the horse deep and canter him on a ten-meter circle until you feel him relax and then collect him again, go off on a line, do another change, put him deep again. Riding the horse deep is very relaxing not only because of the position of the body but also because the horse will associate it with the warming up or cooling down period of a schooling session. I did this with Genaldon when I started pirouettes because he used to freak out. Genaldon loved anything big — flying changes, passage, extensions — anything big where he could be in the air. Anything little where he had to hold his hind legs on the ground — walk-pirouettes, canter pirouettes, piaffe, rein-back — he hated and so when I started the canter pirouettes he started mentally leaving town. I would do a working pirouette for two or three strides and then go on a 20-meter circle and put him deep. Then pick him up for two or three strides of a pirouette, and put him deep again until the tension went away. In time he did fabulous pirouettes.

Jane Savoie

What are the requirements for a correct canter pirouette?

First a horse has to be able to move away from and be controlled by the outside leg. I think a lot of people start on the inside bending way too soon, because they don't take charge with the outside leg and ride the pirouette controlled by outside rein and outside leg even if the bending isn't perfect in the beginning. I think too many people ride a lot of circles, and then when they want to put their outside leg on, the horses stand straight in the air. A horse has to accept the outside leg. A lot of horses don't and are not produced to be supple. So when I make pirouettes, I make them very big. Sometimes I make small circles, large circles like everybody else does. I also like to think that my horse is on what would be a wire wheel and with every stride he takes he must go out to the rim of the wire wheel. He must not only go sideways but he must reach forward with each stride and go to the outside of the rim.

Carol Grant Oldford

A perfect pirouette would be six to seven strides around. It would be basically on the spot behind, the horse jumping in perfect rhythm with his hind legs and maintaining that rhythm through his front end, always three beats, always staying round, bent in the direction of his motion as he goes around. It's a look of absolute harmony where the rider looks like it's just effortless to sit up there and go around in this beautiful pirouette.

Robert Dover

The canter pirouette has the same basic requirements as the pirouette at the walk. The canter has to maintain its three-beat rhythm, the horse has to be slightly bent in the direction of the turn, and the engagement and the balance have to be preserved. It is somewhat easier to prepare the horse for the canter pirouette, since the impulsion of the gait helps to bring the half-halts through. The difficulty for many horses in performing canter pirouettes appears to stem from the combined requirements of strength, balance, and ability to bend the hocks while carrying the rider with a supple back. Horses who have hind leg, especially hock, problems or are weak in the musculature in the back and croup tend to fight this movement like lions. As you make the preparatory half-halts, you can feel them stiffen their back and jaw and "set themselves up" to get this ordeal over with any which way. The problems usually manifest themselves as: haunches falling out, back hollow, head up, speeding up and falling on the rider's inside leg, slowing down and losing canter rhythm or losing the gait entirely, changing leads, and over-turning.

Anne Gribbons

The preparation is important. Then within the pirouette the horse shouldn't lose a great deal of balance. The canter stride should stay true throughout, with the horse thinking of shorter, more active strides. A picture I don't like is when the horse comes to making the pirouette and in collecting slows his body down but then maybe slows his stride down a little too much too, so that by the time he's coming around the last three strides of the pirouette, he's really struggling. I think a lot of work has to be done in making a horse collect a little bit and then making a really collected canter where you keep him a little bit quicker and a little more active and practice making small circles. I sometimes like those better than the spiraling in circles and spiraling out, because I think that if you go down the long side and you make small size circles and really think about the activity of the stride, they help a lot. I have two kinds of exercises that seem to be good. One is to go down the long side (let's say you're on the left lead) and make a half-pirouette to the left, continue up the long side, come a little away from the track and again make a half-pirouette to the left facing the wall. Just make sure that you're not really squashed up against the wall when you start. This exercise is after you're sure he can keep a little activity. The other exercise that I really like a lot once a horse knows pretty much how to make a pirouette is to go across the diagonal and make a pirouette at around about X, continue to the wall and make a half-pirouette. Then come back to X, make your pirouette and then go toward the wall and make your half-pirouette. And you keep going back and forth like that. And that is a wonderful thing for horses that are a bit heavy and strong and don't want to wait in between or after you make the pirouette.

Jessica Ransehousen

What are the most useful exercises to prepare green horses for canter pirouettes?

There are two things that I school quite a bit before actually even attempting a pirouette. One of the main important things is whether the horse can canter on the spot and maintain the quickness of his hind legs and be able to be pushed forward out of that rather than just escaping. The horse has to be very pliable forward and back again with the confidence that he can sit there and canter maybe six steps almost on the spot still thinking in his mind that he's forward. That's probably the most important, and it requires the most strength. When I start to school the pirouette, I don't ever school a complete pirouette the first time. Instead, I make a diamond-figure out in the center of the arena, and at each corner of the diamond I do maybe two steps pirouette and then leave, and then two steps pirouette and then leave so that he allows me to push him out and he allows his hind legs to keep cantering. Then maybe I'll take three or four steps, so that he's still thinking he can leave at any given moment and he never stops and sticks and spins.

Gwen Blake

What I usually do in the beginning is to go on maybe a ten-meter circle, and do haunches-in, but without them starting to turn at all. Just stay on the ten-meter circle, keeping a nice rhythm, keeping the horse's haunches under and really nicely bent to the inside. Once they can do that really well, then I'll start asking them to just sit for a couple of steps and then turn a little and then out of it again. But I never ask for more than a couple of steps. I also do a lot of school canter with them before I start the pirouette. For instance, maybe on a 20-meter circle I'll lengthen the stride and then come back to a really, really collected canter where they just almost canter on the spot for a couple of steps. As soon as they respond I go on again. I do that many times before I start doing pirouettes and then they're really ready. I also do an exercise on a square where I go straight maybe five, six, seven strides and then do a quarter turn onto another straight line, to keep the horses from anticipating and throwing themselves around. And usually I keep them in a little bit of shoulder-in on that line and then the same again — like riding a box. A lot of people start doing a real pirouette too early and then the horses learn to throw themselves around or turn around the middle and panic. If you do it very gradually it works really well and you won't have a problem with it.

Charlotte Bredahl

The reason people have so many difficulties with pirouettes is that they divorce the pirouette from the normal collected canter in their own minds. They start to say, "Okay, now I have a collected canter." Then they come to the pirouette and they ride a completely different way, using their strength, their spurs, their reins, to negotiate the pirouette. What they really should do is work on the half-halts until the horse is able to come easily to a half-halt going on the spot for several strides in the canter, maintaining his balance, maintaining his bend, and maintaining his rhythm and then merely direct that canter anywhere they would like, whether that be a six-meter volte with haunches-in, three-meter or a pirouette that could be used in a Grand Prix test.

The use of shoulder-in and haunches-in and half-pass within the canter just like within the trot produces the same kinds of balance, especially if you're able to half-halt within those different positions that the horse needs in order to be able to do a pirouette. From working shoulder-in and haunches-in and half-pass in the canter, you can start to go on to a volte and produce that same haunches-in. Doing a haunches-in on a volte produces a working pirouette — a working pirouette being possible three to six meters in size with the horse staying in the exact same rhythm as his collected canter, able to half-halt and come on the spot easily and go forward again with ease.

Robert Dover

The horse has to be able to almost canter in place before it can make a pirouette. So preparation for the pirouettes is largely a matter of strength — body building. After collecting the horse as much as possible on a straight line, I then try to ride a half-pass into a small half-circle with the haunches leading slightly. It's important that the horse recognize the pirouette as another collected canter movement where he is allowed to move forward or sideways in a rhythm. Horses are often so held back and pushed, and the canter rhythm so slowed down that they are unable to maintain their balance. They are so confused about what it is that they are being asked to do that they often become disobedient.

Gary Rockwell

To introduce the horse to pirouettes at the canter, spiraling in on the circle until it's a volte or until the canter quality starts to falter, and then allowing the horse to return to the larger size circle is a classic. This exercise also comes in handy when the horse has been laid up and needs to rebuild his "pirouette muscles."

Anne Gribbons

I start by riding haunches-in at the walk and make the horse move up to the outside rein. The outside leg works to make the horse go sideways and forward. I only use my inside leg to get the bend. Then I half-halt both reins simultaneously. I take two steps sideways and two steps forward, and two steps sideways and then go on like that and make bigger and smaller circles. At first, these are not ridden like circles, because the steps are so large, you can't call it a circle. I may even go down the long side a little bit. Then I make smaller and smaller circles until they are in a pirouette. When the horse understands what I mean, then I start to do it in the canter. When I start this work, I always start on the horse's softer side and then go to the stiffer side.

Bent Jensen

What are the most typical mistakes riders make in performing canter pirouettes?

The problems are the same as in walk pirouettes. Basically I don't school a lot of pirouettes. I school the philosophy of a pirouette which is that the rhythm of the canter stays the same and there is bend. Then I ride a volte in haunches-in rather than staying on the same spot. Then as the horse gets stronger and understands what I'm asking, I gradually decrease the size of the circle.

Jane Savoie

This is one of my favorite problems, because I've always had difficulty riding pirouettes. The biggest problem that I've had in learning how to ride pirouettes is to slow down. It has taken me a long time to try to not override and I still do it. Maple Magnum tends to sit down too much in canter pirouettes. In overriding the pirouettes, I plant his hind legs too much on the ground and spin him around trying to make it smaller. We've used a lot of schooling pirouettes, small circles in haunches-in, so that I feel what's going on behind the saddle, and I try to keep the canter rhythm and not be in a hurry to spin him around. Loss of canter rhythm is the greatest problem. The loss of rhythm can cause the horse to spin, walk or trot, or do a flying change out of the pirouette. All due to a loss of balance and rhythm.

Ann Guptill

The horse has to keep stepping behind, has to stay round, and has to stay pushed to the outer rein maintaining inner bend. The horse has to be able to maintain the same tranquil rhythm within the pirouette and the two hind legs have to keep stepping. A lot of times you don't see that. Instead, the horse slams the hind leg and thrusts his upper body up and basically screws himself into the ground and cheats to get himself around. Try to get seven or eight steps to get around in a full pirouette.

Gwen Blake

This is the most difficult canter movement for most horses, because the canter pirouette is the most collected canter movement, and it requires the horse to maintain the same rhythm and tempo of his hind legs as he does in his correct collected canter. Many horses slow the hind legs and don't maintain the throughness. They will resist in the back, poll or jaw. What is important is that the rider feel and maintain the collection of the hind legs into the outside rein and that the horse maintain the correct bend, throughness and speed of the hind legs in the pirouette.

What I feel is a problem in schooling pirouettes is that riders don't balance themselves straight on the horse. They ride too much with the reins, thinking that collection means slowing the horse down. And it's not that at all. It's riding the horse rounder with the horse coming in more collected steps but jumping through with active quick hind legs. The horse has to be ridden from a very light and consistent connection. If we're going to ask the horse to maintain the maximum balance, we have to be riding the maximum balance: a still, quiet seat, very light aids, riding forward into confident, consistent contact.

Kathy Connelly

How do you correct the horse who waits to pivot or stick behind in the half-pirouettes?

The correction for horses that put the hind legs together and lift their front end around with their head and neck is to make the pirouette a little bit bigger and to ride them a little bit deeper, so that they can't pick their front end up so high, and ride them a little more bent to the inside so that the hind legs separate more. The inside hind leg will step more forward and not just slam on the ground very fast. Ride the horse as long and as deep in the neck as you can and still be able to maintain a little canter. In the beginning I do them larger — like a schooling pirouette, so that you don't stress the hind legs so much that they want to cheat to save themselves.

When I can do two or three revolutions in a schooling pirouette, and the horse is comfortable, then I just tighten it up and do a half-pirouette. As I feel the horse tighten his back and want to slam the hind legs down, I get out of it. Each time you school it, see how many more strides you can do on the spot before the horse wants to stiffen and plant his hind legs. Try to add a stride every few days or so until you have a full pirouette.

The easiest way to keep the horse from spinning around is to start with more bend in haunches-in, then open the outside rein, to hold the shoulder back so it doesn't come around so fast.

Horses that step outside and turn on the center, need to do small circles in haunches-in until they are obedient to the outside leg, decreasing the size of the circle as the horse remains on the rider's aids.

Horses that make the pirouette too big either are not strong enough to do the pirouette or are avoiding the difficulty. In the first case, time and strength are the cure. In the second, the rider must demand more so that the horse does not save himself.

Pam Goodrich

What exercises do you do to improve canter pirouettes?

A number of exercises are helpful. It's important before doing canter pirouettes to lengthen and collect, lengthen and collect, feeling the elastic band effect to help engage the hind end and keep a bounding canter. In other words, on 20 meters lengthen maybe six, eight strides and collect again, lengthen six, eight strides and collect again. Travers on a circle is wonderful. The size of the circle depends on the horse's ability to use his back and maintain the correct tempo and rhythm in the hind legs. For example, one can go on 20 meters down to ten meters or eight meters and then make it bigger again. One doesn't do a competition pirouette from travers, but it's a good exercise to strengthen the muscles in the back and hind end. A correctly ridden competition pirouette is done from shoulder-in. It's important that the horse does not run into the rider's inside leg, but rather moves away from the rider's outside leg. The horse must maintain the same degree of consistency in all of the steps — he should not make some steps bigger, some steps smaller. He should not go wide in the first step and then smaller in the following steps. He must always be cantering with ease and with confidence toward the rider's inside leg.

For a horse that speeds up too much and slams into the rider's inside leg, it's better to make bigger working pirouettes where your inside leg is used to teach the horse to slow down and relax into the confidence of the bend. Generally horses who are like that are over-achievers where it's a matter of slowing down the mental training. For these quick thinkers a wonderful exercise is to ride down the quarter markers and then make a box of quarter pirouettes making sure to keep the rhythm of the strides. Another exercise is to do half pirouettes on the diagonal. The diagonal can be as long as is necessary to prepare and collect the horse for the next pirouette. Anther effective exercise to collect the horse is to ride five strides of canter through the corners because the horse must wait and engage coming through the corner.

For a horse that gets wide in his hind legs and doesn't really engage himself, working pirouettes are also good to keep his hind legs quick in the rhythm and not just slow himself down and to maintain engagement.

It's important that the horse learns double pirouette eventually, because they learn the longevity of the pirouette exercise and they don't then lose the engagement in the last two strides of the pirouette and start to get longer and rush out of the pirouette without collection. It's good to ride one single pirouette or two pirouettes, and then ride very collected strides coming out, always with reward. If he makes a mistake, don't punish him, but repeat the exercise with clearer aids. If a horse tries that hard to do something that difficult, then we have to show him the way, not reprimand when he doesn't understand what he did wrong.

Kathy Connelly

If they are getting stuck with the hind legs or bringing their hind legs close together, it means that my outside leg isn't working the horse forward enough. The cure is to go forward out of the pirouette. In the beginning I don't care too much if they come above the bit. I work on that later when the horse has the concept of the pirouette and has the strength in his back and the ability to engage and stay forward in the bridle in the proper carriage and steps.

Bent Jensen

Exercises which are useful to improve on the strength and balance and help the horse to perform the pirouette include: miles of canter at the shoulder-in, half-passes at the canter, cantering inside of the track or on the center line and asking for a half-pirouette at each end of the line, starting with large "schooling" pirouettes and gradually making them smaller.

Anne Gribbons

Gary Rockwell and Suna, at the shoulder-in. Photo by Terri Miller.

I find the zig-zags to be the hardest part of the Grand Prix test. Do you have any advice as to how to ride them?

The zig-zag usually is made more difficult because the rider tries in the flying change itself to produce the first stride of the half-pass to the new direction. This is a mistake. I would come on the centerline. As I straighten the horse on the centerline I will then start to say okay, I'm going to count in my mind one, two begin to straighten on three, and absolutely straight on four. Now in straightening the horse when I had my left leg at the girth, my right leg behind the girth, was sending the horse to the left, my left rein was maintaining the bend to the left, and my right rein was the active rein actually was preventing the horse from just going straight ahead. At the second when I'm straightening the horse, on the third stride I'm going to straighten him by closing my right rein a little more, allowing my left hand to allow the horse to straighten his neck back up. My right leg, which was behind the girth, is going to slide forward, still on the horse. That is the key part of the zig-zag — that you don't take the right leg off the horse when you're going to then jump from the left lead to the right lead. Just like you would do in tempi changes, the inner leg is very important next to the girth because not only does it prevent the horse from drifting into the direction that he is changing into, but because it is the leg that creates impulsion, it produces the expression that you want from that flying change. And so what I do is I say one, two, straighten and. On and, as you say it, you change your aids. You get an absolutely straight flying change which becomes one. Number two will be the first bent stride to the right now. So we go on two, bent and quite sideways and three, bent and quite sideways. On four you are over the centerline again. five, still sideways. Six, still sideways. Seven is just like the stride number three in the first zig-zag. Seven is the straightening — your left leg which was sending the horse sideways begins to slide up the girth, staying on the horse to help him to straight as you close your left hand slightly, just enough to straighten the horse and then on eight, your right rein closes into a fist (that's the half-halt) the right leg going backwards at the same second and your left leg near the girth produces the flying change after the eighth stride. Going back to the left lead, absolutely straight, that's number one. Two, just like the other way, bent. Three, bent. Four, bent over the centerline. Five, bent past the centerline. Six, still bent. Seven, straightening. Eight, absolutely straight, inner leg near the girth, flying change. One, is straight, two, sideways, three, sideways, four, you've arrived on the centerline and you're straight.

Robert Dover

CHAPTER 11

Piaffe and Passage

How do I know when my horse is ready to begin piaffe and passage?

With all my young horses I test to see if it's in them. Some horses may have the physical characteristics needed to do a piaffe but may not be able to handle it mentally. So I try to test them when they're about five and I have a good rider on them. I come behind them and push them a little bit forward in the trot, and I have the rider bring them back on the haunches and usually nine times out of ten if it's in there, it starts to come out from the trot.

I tested both Juvel and Darien before I bought them. So many people look at the conformation of a horse and say "He should be able to do this and he should be able to do that," but I think more times than not, there are horses that don't seem to have the mechanics for doing piaffe and passage and yet end up doing them. So the conformation that I look for isn't as important as what's in the horse's mind. If he has the tendency to lower the croup when tapped on by the rider, he'll catch on just fine.

Gwen Blake

When the introduction of these movements takes place in relation to the horse's training is entirely up to the horse. There are horses which are physically strong enough and sufficiently mature mentally to start as soon as they show some collection and can carry themselves under the rider at all gaits. Like good pirouettes and one-tempis, the piaffe and/or passage are the ingredients that can make or break a Grand Prix horse. I have met horses who panic at the thought of having to "trot in place" and who can never accept the concept. The non-teachable ones I have observed fall into two basic categories: the horses with hock and/or back problems who experience physical pain when attempting to piaffe, and the ones who are claustrophobic and cannot handle the "stop-and-go" requirement. The former type can possibly be helped with physical therapy, while the latter is always an accident waiting to happen. I have seen perfectly reasonable animals become completely frantic and flip over or freeze at the mere suggestion of a piaffe. Some of these disasters could be due to incorrect training, but not all. There are horses who simply cannot learn to piaffe, even when they are properly introduced to the movement. The other side of the coin are the naturals who appear to be dying for you to ask for a piaffe. This kind comes with built-in rhythm and ability to lower their haunches and bend their hocks. I helped train one horse which displayed this talent before I bought him as an unbroken three-year-old. He would gallop up to the gate, stop short and just stand there in the mud, exhibiting a near-perfect piaffe without a rider. When nobody came to bring him in, he passaged around until he got some attention. Sure enough, his strongest points as a Grand Prix horse were the piaffe and passage. Not all horses who behave this way in freedom perform as well under a rider, but I'd say your odds are good that they will.

Anne Gribbons

Do you start piaffe or passage first?

I've found that horses with a huge trot do better starting with the piaffe first in part in order to begin regulating the huge trot into a smaller, active gait on command. It encourages the big-moving horse to learn about lift-up and down movement.

The horse with a smaller trot will probably find the piaffe easy at a later stage, but introduction of passage first will encourage a bigger, forward balance into the trot. Of course this is a general theory — there are exceptions.

Gary Rockwell

I've not come across a horse that needs to learn the passage before the piaffe. I think that because the piaffe is your tool for collection that you're going to need, on most horses, to teach it first. I've always taught piaffe first, because too often, you'll see a floaty trot that's not really on the aids that can be misunderstood for a passage-y trot. You want to teach that horse to collect and to be sharp to the rider's aids and to be able to hold that collection with active hind legs. Piaffe is a wonderful tool for teaching the horse to hold that collection. Piaffe can be a wonderful schooling aid, because it teaches the horse that he can be that forward and yet not cover ground. To be able to hold that kind of collection, to have that kind of power and stay in one place is a major concept for a horse that you want to be an FEI horse.

Ann Guptill

I generally train the piaffe first. That's not to say that it is a universal rule because I don't believe in universal rules for horses or for people. If you have a scenario where the horse accepts the idea of piaffing from the very beginning, and has a natural great ability to piaffe but has less of an ability to produce a long period of suspension and a thrusting forward into the air, which would produce a beautiful passage or an extended trot from that passage, then it can be better to just hold off, knowing that the piaffe is there waiting for you. You'd then work on the idea of a cadenced passage that the extended trot can be enhanced by and half-passes and all collected trot can be enhanced by as well. Generally horses normally should learn piaffe first and then from the piaffe, from that understanding of engaging and being rhythmic behind and supple and trotting truly on the spot, then we allow that to move forward and we train them to the passage as well.

Robert Dover

A lot of times I have found that if one teaches the passage first it keeps the horse's hind legs farther out behind him. I don't think the passage is that difficult to train after the horse has learned to engage and come under through the piaffe.

Gwen Blake

In general, passage, particularly with warmblood horses, is a very easy thing to train, and I think it can be a little bit dangerous particularly with the very big movers if they learn passage before piaffe. So 99% of the time I will not teach passage or even introduce it until the piaffe is pretty well established. However, I worked with a couple of horses who have flat trots — something seen in a lot of Thoroughbreds — and I have introduced passage quite early to try and develop more suspension and a stronger back for collection, but that is really the only time that I would consider teaching passage first.

Belinda Nairn

I prefer to teach the piaffe first, since some horses with a lot of natural suspension who "like" to passage tend to defend themselves against true collection by bouncing around in passage. However, there are horses who find it easier to develop the piaffe out of the passage. A gradually shortened passage can be transformed into a piaffe for a few strides and then resumed. At times the trot has proved to me to be the connecting gait from which the horse learned both the piaffe and the passage, especially in the case of horses who tend to get stuck in either movement.

Ann Gribbons

A little bit together. Again in the passage, I like to bring the horse back and activate the trot, first at a somewhat slower rhythm and then push him forward and then bring him back and push him a little bit and try to get it that way. There are some horses that naturally are easier than others. Orphie was not easy. I just am not very keen about spending a lot of time with a long whip with somebody going behind, because I'm a little nervous about what happens to a lot of horses when you step away. I'd rather that they were listening more to the rider's legs and not relying too much on the long whip.

Jessica Ransehousen

Almost always piaffe. I've run into situations where it has been so totally clear in my mind that I would never teach passage first. With Evidence, who tended to have a swimmy trot, I knew he would love to do circus passage where he would push off his hind legs. I knew to not even touch passage until he learned to sit and carry weight behind from learning piaffe.

Jane Savoie

I always teach piaffe first. Piaffe is trot on or near the spot. Because in the learning stages, the horse is not strong enough, there is little or no suspension. That increases as the horse gets stronger. Passage has a great deal of suspension. If taught first, when asked to do it almost on the spot, it's too hard, and the horse has difficulty understanding what the rider wants. Conversely, the idea of building a bigger more suspended stride from piaffe is not as difficult. It's similar to what they have been doing in half-halts.

The prerequisites for a piaffe are that the horse has to understand the concept of all the lateral movements — even if they're not perfect — has to be able to do the rein-back quietly and correctly, and has to be able to take a simple half-halt. I start it many ways. Most of the warmbloods I start in hand first, because it's just easier to have the person in front as a wall in front of them. With most of the Thoroughbred types, I've had more success by doing it on top of the horse, because they get too nervous without the rider's aids to reassure them. Most Thoroughbred types have difficulty in the walk, and I find that they have trouble finding the rhythm in the piaffe. With them it's easier to slow the trot to help show them the piaffe rhythm.

The warmbloods I do from halt because they take such big strides that they tend to push right through the rider. I teach them in hand from halt to stay in one spot and move their legs and not bull through me. This is much easier to do on the ground because you're in front of them — you can tell them they have to stay there without pulling on the reins. If you pull on the reins, you stop or inhibit the hind legs. I don't do a lot of long lining only because I tend to either have Thoroughbred types or huge tanks that drag me around.

Pam Goodrich

I always teach piaffe first. I never let the horse do passage until they piaffe, because excellent transitions come from teaching piaffe first and being able to have the power to spring into passage and back. If you teach the passage, sometimes the talented horse uses that too often against you.

Carol Grant Oldford

When do you introduce piaffe?

I generally start the horses in hand because I trust my sight better than I trust my feel and I don't want to create problems. And I really enjoy it. It's like a jigsaw puzzle — you put it in a piece at a time until you have the final picture. When you first start the work in hand piaffe is almost unrecognizable. All you do is touch the horse with a stick on one hind leg and if he picks it up, he gets a sugar and a 'good boy.' So it starts with a step like that and it's fun to see it evolve. If I'm by myself and I don't have a ground-person, I will do a mounted exercise where I'm laying a foundation for piaffe. I avoid problems by making it very clear to the horse that piaffe is trot. We do a lot of transitions from collected trot to half-steps where I decrease the amount of ground covered by maybe 50 percent but maintain the same activity. And as long as I ride collected trot, half-steps, collected trot, half-steps and no less forward than that, I know that I'm not doing anything where I could get into trouble later down the road.

Jane Savoie

I believe in not riding a horse at all before he's four. I never have and I don't plan to either. I think you make up for the time at the other end if you wait until later. I have a six-year-old now that was green broke at four and a half and I started teaching him a little bit of piaffe when he was five and a half but only driving which is how I teach my horses. I'm comfortable with that because I've done a lot of driving of horses. I have a surcingle and side reins on them and I usually lunge them first. Then I put the two lunge lines attached to the surcingle onto the bit and then I usually go down a wall or by a fence and try just to keep them straight. I pretend I'm going to make them stop, but then before they stop, I activate them with the whip, and then at the same time, I release the reins the minute they start coming back. If they can get a few half-steps, I'm happy, and I reward them. I want them to really think forward. And then as soon as they respond, I ask them to trot forward again. I think I start probably a little bit early, but I go very slowly, and I don't demand a lot for a long time.

My six-year-old can actually do quite a bit of piaffe. It's something I practice maybe once a week driving him. I'll do a little bit of passage but I don't do piaffe on his back, because I really don't feel he's strong enough. And I think it's better that he gets really, really confirmed with the piaffe while I am driving him because it's easier for him without my weight. I won't do it on his back until it looks like it's really easy for him. Sometimes a horse will offer piaffe or passage when I'm on his back. I don't think that's bad: I let them do it. And when I do it on his back, I have a ground person and I do the piaffe really forward from trot, not from walk. I don't like to do it from walk, because I've seen too many horses anticipate the piaffe out of the walk and then it really ruins the walk. A lot of horses will start getting lateral, because they know you might ask for the piaffe. You start collecting the walk and they right away think piaffe and you don't have a walk anymore. For that reason I never piaffe from the walk.

Charlotte Bredahl

Usually by five, after they're accepted the aids, the horse can piaffe in hand with a rider at his head and the rider sitting on his back with a little help possible or maybe no help. The first thing I do is have someone hold them in hand with the lunge line and a cavesson over a bridle and sometimes light side reins, sometimes not. Then I make sure that first I've taught the horse to bring each leg forward by the use of the whip. It's not piaffe yet — it's only that he will move his leg — not go against my stick. Then I teach him to trot forward (and the person on the ground has to run backwards) and that when I cluck he has to really trot. And then of course by this time they're running over the ground person and the ground person (and I have someone really good) stops the horse when he runs over the hand and then he learns to stop in the front. Then pretty soon the 'go' and 'stop' is organized, and he's not kicking at the stick and you can cluck and usually the talented ones will do a few steps in three weeks.

Carol Grant Oldford

As in all training, I think it's important to learn from the horse and to evaluate each horse individually. Remember that what's most important about training the piaffe is how you begin it, because you are creating the lifetime impression for the horse of what is to be expected of him. The piaffe is probably the most difficult movement for the horse to do in the trot as canter pirouettes are the most difficult for most horses in the canter, because they require the greatest degree of collection.

I like to train my horses to work in hand on the long lines and do some driving with them. I've had the great fortune to work with Ernst Bachinger from the Spanish Riding School. He is a true master at this, and I've watched him perform miracles in just a few days with horses. (Bachinger did the exhibition of long lining at the 1972 Olympics in Munich.) For work in hand, you need a strong handler who can deal with the exuberant or aggressive horse who might try to run through the bridle. The horse must be obedient to the bridle and also the person who is handling the long lines and the whip must be clever and skillful in order to train the horse correctly about his hind legs so that the horse can learn the rhythm of the piaffe and also be willingly responsive. It's a matter of time and experience to gain that kind of cleverness and know where and when to touch the horse, and when to be rewarding and when to be more demanding. Clucking is also an important voice aid in training piaffe. Ultimately, it must come to the point where a quiet cluck with quiet seat and leg aids and no whip exact an active piaffe. Eventually no cluck is needed. What's most important is that fear is not used, because when fear is introduced it's only a matter of time until there will be some aberration in the piaffe. This is often irreparable. Once the horse has learned the rhythm of the piaffe in the long lines I'll sometimes take him out two times a day from the stall and long line him for just a short period of time, always making it fun, always making it rewarding and trying to train into him a high self-esteem. If a horse thinks he's good at something then he wants to do it. If he thinks he's not good at it, just like us, he doesn't want to do it.

If a horse is very tense or fearful, especially if he is fearful of whips from some past experience, it may be much better to begin piaffe on the horse's back, rather than in hand.

I think that it's important that the horse learn in the natural progression of the trot work, how to maintain the rhythm in the trot in the collected steps that lead up to the piaffe. It's important that the rider keep the horse very alive to the leg, very, very light to the leg. In piaffe, and also in canter pirouettes, the rider would like to be able to use the lightest leg possible on the horse in order to get these very collected movements instead of using a strong leg to get these movements and squeezing harder and finally kicking at the horse for a more active piaffe or pirouette. Eventually the overactive leg aid deadens a horse to the leg. I would use the analogy of a soft voice versus a shouting voice. The horse must learn always to listen to the soft voice, light leg, rather than the shouting voice, i.e. the kicking leg. Again, it's important to understand how to do less to get more. I think this is a very important stimulus response to train into the horse from the first moment the rider introduces the horse to piaffe.

We can't discuss piaffe without discussing the quality of the trot. The piaffe is the most collected trot. It's trot on the spot with maximum impulsion and cadence, and it must maintain the two-beat rhythm of the trot. The rider must be aware in all the trot work of maintaining the relaxation and suppleness of the elastic band effect, working the horse in the different trots, always forward and through and straight into the bridle. The rider should not let the horse go sideways with his hind legs and not allow him to hollow or drop his back but ride him into a soft, elastic, supple and rewarding hand from a firm and quiet seat. The rider should be aware of not letting the horse's hind legs slow down but rather of maintaining a very active hind leg. I use different approaches, depending on the horse, to teach piaffe from the saddle.

Piaffe can be trained from the walk. However, it should be done with caution because it can affect the purity of the walk. If the horse has some tendency for tenseness as he's learning piaffe and simultaneously has tendency for a pacey or two-beat rhythm in the walk it can be dangerous because the two-beat rhythm of the piaffe can affect the four-beat rhythm of the walk.

Piaffe can also be trained from the trot. I begin with very collected steps, with trot half steps that are very active and then ride forward again. I ride just a few steps so that the horse learns to step under and learns to feel comfortable bearing his weight behind and pushing himself forward again straight into the reins without slowing the hind legs as he becomes more collected.

It's important that the rider always rewards the horse's efforts to come forward and through into the bridle and does not punish him for the mistakes that he will naturally make in his efforts to try to do this exercise. It's important that we keep it fun, and that we use lots of rewards so that the horse develops and maintains a desire to piaffe.

Kathy Connelly

I think in some cases, anyway, that horses can deal with only one major learning process at a time. For instance, learning flying changes really takes up everything the horse has at that time. Usually after the flying changes I like to spend a lot of time doing trot and collecting the trot to the walk transition, taking the horse quite under and making him very active into the walk, and then picking up the trot again and really getting him alive to the leg. It isn't really piaffe at the start — just that little ability to compress and still keep the trot stride. This is long before it looks like anything. This also really helps the collected trot. Then when you are expecting to do more steps, the horse is much more active to your leg. When Orpheus first began piaffe, he was so quick and I had a lot of trouble and that's why I did it from the trot because it was really helpful to him to just keep him thinking of trot.

Jessica Ransehousen

I vary it according to the horse, and as I learn more about piaffe, I'm starting to introduce it to horses at a much younger age. I used to have the philosophy that the horse had to have all the basic requirements of an FEI horse before you would think of introducing a movement that technically involves such collection. But what I have found with some horses is that when you introduce such a difficult movement later in their training and they have absolutely no familiarity with it, it can become a big issue and a difficult thing to teach. This seems to hold true with a lot of horses, particularly warmblood horses, so what I'm doing more now is introducing half steps at a younger age and not demanding the kind of collection that you would expect of an upper level horse, but at least introducing the concept and the idea of holding the trot back and maintaining little half steps. I vary with whether I introduce it in hand or on top of the horse. In general I would say that I do it from on top of the horse. Again that seems to be a little bit more of a natural thing for them and they seem to accept it well. However, if I have decent help from the ground, that can be a good introduction also.

Starting the piaffe work with Christopher was actually quite easy, as Christopher was such a natural athlete, as well as a sensitive, responsive horse. His natural offering was so correct, that there was little I had to do as far as development. However, the risk with a horse like him, was that because these movements were so easy and natural for him, he would and could do so much without clearly understanding and honestly accepting what he was doing. This made him a real intellectual ride, and was a great lesson to me in understanding the importance of being honestly on the aids.

Belinda Nairn

Can you discuss your method of teaching piaffe/passage in hand?

Once again I have no rules for this. There are some horses that I work extensively in hand with. Some of these horses are Jonathan Livingstone Seagull, who learned the piaffe not only in hand but with a halter and a lead rope on him. With the horse that I'm competing on now, Electron, I am doing a lot of work from the ground, and I will maintain that through the entire spring and summer. But, with most horses, I also do work from the saddle. With some horses who come to a piaffe and passage with ease I just work from the saddle. I think that all the different uses of working in hand as well as working from the saddle can be very, very profitable to the rider and horse and the most important thing throughout is that you maintain the horse's love for what he is doing — that he comes to the piaffe and the passage looking at it as a game that he enjoys.

Robert Dover

I make the transition from work in hand to work under saddle by finding a common denominator. When working in hand, I will cluck in rhythm and then when I first start on the horse's back, clucking becomes the common denominator. In this way they understand that what they are being asked for from the saddle is the same as what they are being asked for from the ground. I try very hard not to use the cluck carelessly. I save my cluck for important things like schooling piaffe because that's going to be my common denominator when I transfer from work in hand to under saddle.

Jane Savoie

If the rider is experienced, I prefer to start with the rider mounted. This gives the horse an easier "out" if he become nervous, and at the same time he cannot break away and leave the scene as sometimes happens when you work a horse in hand and he becomes tense or angry. A few steps at a time, with plenty of time for praise in between is all you want. The person on the ground has to be experienced, and the rider has to know that the whip will never touch the horse if he is about to panic. Few things are worse than being mounted on a confused horse and not trusting the ground person to know when NOT to use the whip. Bad timing or overzealousness from the person on the ground can ruin things for good! If the horse does not understand the concept, no amount of whip aids are going to produce a piaffe. It may take a less talented or slow-thinking animal weeks, perhaps months, to figure out what the game is. A little bit every day is the best way to slip it into his daily routine. The more of a big deal you make, the more suspicious the horse tends to get. Some horses are so sensitive that the mere thought of someone behind them with a whip makes them unable to focus. The good news is that such a horse usually does not need much work from the ground, but can be taught from the saddle alone.

Anne Gribbons

When doing work in hand, I am next to the horse's head and use a whip in the rear, because I've found that horses have trouble concentrating on too many people. They have a much easier time concentrating on one person. If they want to run through me I rap them right on the soft part of their nose or their chest with a whip. They learn right from the beginning that they can't run over me. That's a first prerequisite and I'll spend as many days as necessary doing walk, halt, walk, halt on the wall. Once they learn that, when I activate them, I remind them as often as necessary until they stay and control their energy without bolting forward. And if they get going too much I just stop and I'll do maybe a little rein back, go forward and start over again.

Pam Goodrich

I don't work very much in hand. I've had a few horses that got the piaffe rhythm easier in hand than they did with the rider on, but I usually try from the saddle. In the end, I want the horse to piaffe from what is initially a trot aid, so that's why I don't train it. Most of all, I don't want a horse to rely on the whip in the teaching of the piaffe. That's where a lot of people go wrong. They teach it with the whip, they ride it with the whip, and then they can't get it in the show ring without a whip.

Gary Rockwell

I think every horse tells you something different. Every horse reacts differently to how you use the whip, and I think you really have to sort of feel your way. Some horses you touch them on the butt and that works, and some horses you touch the hocks. A lot of it depends on where they need help. A lot of horses will use one hind leg more than the other and then you only need to touch the one hind leg. Some of them don't pick up their front feet, and you need to touch their front leg — it just totally depends on the horse, I think.

Charlotte Bredahl

What do you like to see achieved in-hand before you start to get on the horse's back to do the piaffe work?

I put somebody on when I can walk up to the wall and click my tongue and maybe give one tap with the whip and the horse piaffes. When I put a rider up there basically I do exactly as if there was no rider up there. I stand by the horse and let the rider give a little touch with the whip and then what I do is I back away but always stay close to reinforce so that the rider doesn't have to do very much until he or she can just take over. And again how much I stand behind the horse depends on each horse. Some horses get really afraid of that. On the other hand, there are horses that are not afraid and tend to know, "Aha, the person is not there, I don't need to piaffe." I don't want the rider to do too much, with horses like that at this stage, if the rider has to start out doing too much, the same will happen in the arena. I stand right behind the horse with a lunge whip so that he can't see me and he never knows if I'm there or not and he never knows if the whip is going to be there or not. And that way the horse learns that he has to keep going. But you have to know the horse. You could do that with some horses, and they become so strong and nervous that it's deadly. And on another horse it's all right. It depends on the horse.

Pam Goodrich

I put an experienced rider on him who knows if the horse is a little behind the aids to send him forward immediately before I even notice it. And I don't do too much with the stick because by that time they're in front of my stick, but I might just possibly touch the outside hind leg standing in a driving position. If the horse becomes balky at all to the stick, I have the rider send him into a nice brisk forward trot or canter. And then pretty soon we collect the walk a little bit more when he's really in front of the stick and pretty soon I might cluck and he will go forward and again the talented ones are already in piaffe. You have the occasional horse that will want to come at you. We take a little more time with them on the ground so that they again understand the sticks. It's also a point also of balance.

The tendency of the talented horse is to get too quick and to do what I call stumble over their front end and they do that so that they don't stand on their hind legs. They lift their hips up too high. That may be the beginning of going too wide. So even if my horses stop and don't piaffe I want their weight to be on their hind legs. So they may be stuck and maybe they'll stop cold and stand there. Then we just briskly trot forward so that they get the idea they have to come under and stand on their hind legs. I think the first part of teaching piaffe is critical or they learn it too late almost.

Carol Grant Oldford

What exercises do you use to teach passage?

I think a big problem for many horses or riders is that they shorten it up too much and the horses are not forward. I have found it helpful to do a lot of passage into trot or maybe medium trot, just a few steps, just enough for the horse to think he's going somewhere and then back to passage. And then I do walk-passage

Jane Savoie with Zapatero, in piaffe. Photo by Mary Phelps.

transitions but only for a few steps of passage. If they come up into good passage then back to walk again. I do a lot of transitions without holding the passage for very long until I feel they're really strong. If you get some really good steps, fine. Reward him this way. They don't have a chance to really get tired and then again, they don't dread it so much. Even when they get stronger, it should be a very gradual thing. In the beginning I'll only do maybe five, ten steps of passage and then out of it again and then back in again. And as they get stronger, then you can do it closer together and for longer periods, but never to the point that they get tired. Sometimes I think it works well if you go out and work on the trail if you have a lazy horse. You go out on a trail, and on your way home you ask him; you always have more impulsion when you're out of the ring.

Charlotte Bredahl

I think passage is easier to train sometimes than piaffe, because every horse can trot and from that trot you can build a passage. Obviously the horse that has a great deal of suspension is going to have a much easier time learning the passage than the horse that has a very flat trot. When a horse has a flat trot, it's important to develop his muscular structure to try to build in more strength so that he can develop and sustain the suspension. This can be done through the suppling work, through correctly ridden lateral work, and with certain specific exercises. For example, riding passades. Begin with riding half circles in the trot and decrease the size of the half circle as long as the horse is able to maintain the rhythm and tempo. Eventually as he becomes stronger it will be the size of a passade. With half-passes, the horse develops and matures in his ability to maintain the balance and the rhythm of the half-pass. You can increase the angle and go very sideways. This should always be done with the horse being ridden well into the rider's inside leg so that he's really maintaining the impulsion and the balance on the hind end and not falling on the inside shoulder. It also is helpful in developing both piaffe and passage to do this kind of suppling work in the walk. You can do half-passes in the walk alternating to leg yield. For example, you may start in a right half-pass, coming across K X M, and then you may change the bend to leg yield as you continue across the diagonal in the walk or the trot and then change the bend back to the half-pass. This should be done not in a staccato motion, but giving the horse a chance to balance himself and maintain the weight on his hind quarters. Always ride the horse straight in between your change of bend from the leg yield and back to the half-pass and vice versa.

What is important in training passage is that the horse is ridden straight into the reins and always ridden forward and through into the bridle. Horses that have a great deal of suspension in their trot can sometimes learn an incorrect passage, because they can learn not to close the hind legs underneath them but rather to keep them out behind them. An inexperienced rider will sometimes think he is passaging, because there's a great deal of suspension and yet there will not be the engagement behind, and the horse will not have the ability to lower his hindquarters for transition to piaffe because the engagement is not there. Evidence of correct engagement is ease in the piaffe-passage transitions.

Kathy Connelly

I have used something that produces a little bit of noise like a light bamboo pole on the knees of the horse. It is carried just above the knees and as the horse comes up with each front leg, he hits the pole. The sound of it more than anything else encourages the horse to pick his legs up higher. Trotting poles would be a possibility although I haven't actually ever had to do that. I've been fortunate. I haven't really run into a lot of horses that I've had difficulty with but I did use a bamboo pole with Jolicoeur to make his passage bigger, and that was helpful. Zapatero had fabulous passage, but he had really no piaffe to speak of. Part of it was lack of understanding. Mostly it was lack of strength. He did an unrecognizable piaffe where he walked with the hind legs and crossed them like tightrope walking. The biggest training challenge with him has been first to teach him to widen his hind legs rather than cross and then over time develop the strength so that he could do so easily.

Jane Savoie

You can go back to the cavalletti so they learn how to pick their forearm up and hind leg together. A tool that I got from Pam Goodrich is the Spanish Walk. I've used it on a few horses, and it teaches the horse how to be able to lift the forearm and shoulder, if the horse doesn't have that kind of lift by nature.

Ann Guptill

For Percy it was very hard. I had to wait and wait in the piaffe, wait and wait until finally he learned to push himself out of that piaffe into the passage. And that was strength. And again they have to weight their hind legs and use their back and not get quick. Some horses don't use their backs very easily and Percy was one of those horses. So you very much have to think that suppleness and balance have to really be there.

Carol Grant Oldford

How do you maintain straightness in passage?

In passage, when you're crooked in the air and crooked on landing, you're apt to try to correct only on landing. There's only a split second when two feet are on the ground and the other two feet are in the air and then everything's in the air all at once and now what? So I try to correct the passage by turning on circles. Currently, I have my crookedness at passage even better corrected by finally being able to do passage half-pass. I can really control the crookedness, now, because I have control of the hind legs and the shoulders together in the half-pass. Now I can go straight on a much more collected horse. His hind legs are farther under his body than they have ever been before, because when he's not underneath himself he cannot do passage half-pass. I was not able to do it for three straight years. I am still trying. He would roll sideways from shoulder to shoulder, called balancé, which is just an on-the-forehand evasion of going straight forward to the bit. That could be called crookedness but it's really something else. Half-pass makes the job very difficult for him to balance and turning on circles makes him become more connected. I can remember when I couldn't turn in passage at all.

Carol Lavell

So many horses seem to "burn out" in piaffe and passage and to lose the quality of these movements. How do you maintain the freshness and avoid the "jet lag piaffe"?

My philosophy when it comes to training piaffe and passage has come to be never to try to force the issue. If the horse has talent, he'll come around and even be proud to show his parade number. In the piaffe in particular, it is important that the horse has fun showing off and is not displaying "fear in place." Some lazy horses never have fun doing anything that involves moving their bodies, and they will undoubtedly need some strong "encouragement." But ambitious horses do not need to be pressured, just shown the way. I have seen world renowned trainers fail to teach either piaffe or passage to a horse, because the animal just could not mentally grasp the concept or did not have the physical equipment to perform one or the other. Every horse is not destined to reach Grand Prix, no matter how cleverly we operate. If you have a horse who performs both piaffe and passage reasonably well and, even better, the very difficult transitions between the two, keep him fresh by not over-training. Short and happy sessions with plenty of praise will keep him anxious to show off his piaffe and passage in the ring which is where you need it!

Anne Gribbons

I try to keep them thinking that they're trotting and not let them think that it's a bigger thing than that. It's not a movement but a way to think of it in his mind. So they don't shut off.

Gwen Blake

This is where I believe that you never stop doing your trot collections and doing your forward piaffe steps out of the trot. Never give that up, because you can do a lot of work in the Grand Prix. You can take that movement and you can ride it trot instead of passage and your activation out of the trot to forward piaffe step instead of piaffe and just do a lot of that. The horse never really gets so dead to your legs. You know I think sometimes people practice too much passage to piaffe and piaffe to passage. I think it's important to do a lot of this sort of activation work and try to keep him active and marching forward. I think you have never to forget that you want to keep the horse alive to your leg. Do it within the trot work, because you can correct the trot work, but it's really hard to correct the horse over and over again in the piaffe. It should be saved as being something more special, especially after he knows it. And you know, women are not as strong as men so therefore we need to use little other things to keep them happy and going. A lot of people do different things to get passage and in the end it's kind of yank and crank for awhile.

Jessica Ransehousen

I think too many horses are drilled too much, and that's why they hate it. They're made to just do piaffe and piaffe and piaffe, and they get absolutely sick of it. And too much whip, too much all kinds of equipment, and they're not rewarded for it when they do it. They're asked to do more and more and more. And so they only time they do get back at you is in the ring, and that's what they do. Some horses are just lazy, and they will quit on you in the ring no matter how you do it, and I don't think there's much hope to really fix that. Once they've learned to quit, it's a very, very difficult problem. I don't do a lot of it with my horses.

Charlotte Bredahl

Once a horse is confirmed in piaffe and is competing at the Grand Prix level, my basic philosophy is that less becomes more. The most important thing in a confirmed Grand Prix horse is to preserve their talent and willingness, not destroy it. I like to vary their training program a lot with hacking, and using the natural terrain to keep them fit. I don't drill the piaffe every day. Some days I will warm the horse up and only do piaffe and passage, and the next day will only do canter work. Doing a little piaffe going down a hill is a tremendous strengthening exercise, and still allows the horse a change. Having a fresh mind becomes my main focus and I will vary the program accordingly.

Belinda Nairn

It's very, very difficult to produce a Grand Prix horse and maintain that same quality of freshness that he had when he first began the Grand Prix. Likewise, you also have the problem with nerves when horses do start Grand Prix. It may take a year or two for them to settle into that level and feel that they are comfortable doing this piaffe passage work. I think that what you need to do is not expect the horse in his very first Grand Prix season to do the Olympic Gold Medal piaffe-passage tour. If it happens, then great. If it doesn't happen, one shouldn't go wild and start making the horse piaffe 150 steps on the spot again and again because that will make him lose both his nerve, his desire, and unfortunately, many times it makes him lose his soundness. So, when you have a very talented horse, one thing I think is important is that if you get into the test and you find that you have a nice passage to a nice piaffe but it's inching forward and you'll probably end up with a five or a six, take that in the perspective of where you are with that horse that season and then say to yourself, "I'm going to work on having the horse be able to find his balance from passage to piaffe, staying on the spot, understanding he's trotting all the time, and then move back to passage in an easy way." It's something that has to evolve over time and when riders really mess up it's usually because they're not taking into consideration that necessary evolution over time. They want it now — they want it immediately — they judge it to be imperfect unless it is exactly what would classically be written down into a book.

Robert Dover

So much depends on the horse. So much depends on how much pressure the horse can take. Horses that can take quite a bit of pressure often have a little bit of a slow engine which needs a little revving up. So day to day I make sure that they are really, really sensitive to the legs and that they do a really super piaffe no matter where I am. If they don't, they get nailed with the leg or the whip. Now a lot of the German horses get a little ticked off at that and they start swelling up and resenting it. A lot of horses resent it. You have to be a lot more clever on how you approach those horses, meaning that they have to really like it, they have to know they're going to get in trouble if they don't. But really — it has to be something that they really like to do.

A lot of it has to do with connection. This is a very difficult thing to describe, because piaffe is two things; it starts out with a trick. It turns into trot on the spot and trot on the spot has all the characteristics of trot moving as far as suspension to the back, connection with the reins, etc. The problem is that not all horses can do that. It's a really special horse that can do that — a Rembrandt. The problem that most horses have in piaffe in the arena when they don't do enough is that they have trouble piaffing or trotting on the spot. Consequently it is a trick and they learn they don't have to do the trick in the arena. If you have a horse that is not the super athlete, it takes a real clever rider to have the horse want to do the trick in the arena and it means being conscious not to over push them. Each horse is so different as to how far you can push them without driving them over the edge or not pushing them enough so that they don't do it at all. One thing you can do when they start doing it quite well at home all the time, is to take them away and do a mock show. Put on your outfit, and prepare it as if you were going to do the test and make the same correction that you do at home and stand there until they do it. You do that until when you go away from home all dressed up in the suit, they don't know it's a show. They go in the arena assuming that they're going to get the correction so they might as well just do it just like they do at home.

Pam Goodrich

I would not ride with a stick in practice. And when they quit I just send them forward (into the trot) every time until they're really in front of my legs and lots of reward. I think a horse who quits has lost his desire. Not all horses can do it. You can tell that when you start the piaffe — some can do it so easily and for other ones it's not part of their nature. They may be very good Prix St. Georges horses. I've taken some further than Prix St. Georges which I should not have, and I think you make them suffer if you go beyond that.

Carol Grant Oldford

It's important for the longevity and maintenance of the piaffe that a horse's desire to do it is worked with as carefully as his ability to do it. One mistake that's made in the training of piaffe is that riders drill it too much, and tend to practice it when a horse is tired. Intersperse the piaffe with the other work — do it in the beginning and middle of the sessions when he is not so tired. I think it's important that we listen to what the horse's reactions are so that we work the piaffe at a time when he's fresh and relaxed and not once he's very tired. Once a horse has learned the piaffe steps in long lines and responds without the whip but simply to a cluck, it's time to put a rider on the horse's back. This should be a rider who can maintain the balance with the horse very easily and who has a deep yet relaxed seat and can be riding the horse forward and straight into the reins. It is important that the rider not interfere in the reins with the horse's balance. With the use of light leg aids for the piaffe it should be, as on the ground, simply that the rider can cluck and get a few steps. One of the problems that comes in training piaffe is that one can be too demanding at certain points with horses when they're still figuring it out. It's more important that they are rewarded for doing a few steps, than that we try to create the perfect Olympic piaffe in the beginning when they are still learning the very basic 'how to.' I work my horses in the long lines and driving even after they know the piaffe under saddle because I feel that the interplay of the two helps to maintain a suppleness and makes it a lot of fun for the horse. Generally, horses that have been trained in hand, really like to work in hand on the long lines. I also practice the piaffe out on the trail always with reward, not making it the grand moment of possible force and failure but something that's fun for them to do and that they develop an earnest desire to perform again.

I always do something after I work on piaffe when I'm riding. I don't just end with that. I feel that it's important for the horse to think of it as just part of his regular work session, not as the big moment that creates anxiety. After I work piaffe I always do something else, and if I'm schooling a test and doing the last centerline of the Grand Prix I always ride on and do something else from there, so he doesn't think that it's just over. Otherwise it may be difficult for a horse that is in the Grand Prix test time after time, to sustain a piaffe and the passage work on the last centerline. So only in competition do I end with those movements. I think that it is important that we keep doing activation work in the trot in order to keep the piaffe sustained over a long period of time. It's good to work piaffe-passage, piaffe-passage, piaffe-passage transitions, but also school trot-piaffe-trot transitions to maintain the activation in the trot work and therefore also in the piaffe.

Kathy Connelly

What can you tell me about the piaffe-passage transition?

Initially they were difficult for Zapatero because the piaffe was in an evolutionary period. To improve the transitions, I needed to feel the passage in the piaffe and the piaffe in the passage. They were really one and the same; they were within each other. And that has probably helped me to help him more than anything else, I'm passaging on the spot now, therefore, I'm piaffing. And then I'm piaffing forward, therefore, I'm passaging.

Jane Savoie

The upward transition from piaffe to passage is more difficult for me with Maple Magnum because he sits too much in the piaffe. It's easier for me to ask him to collect the passage and then piaffe.

Ann Guptill

I think they're both very difficult and I think they both require the same type of balance and they have to keep the rhythm coming in and going out which requires an incredible amount of strength and balance. In the beginning with a green Grand Prix horse, what I've found that has helped the horse and helped me school the transition, is to take the piaffe and travel with it so it really wasn't a piaffe on the spot and it wasn't really passage — it was a moving piaffe or a passage on the spot. So I got the horse to really feel those steps of the transition and I found it to be extremely useful in the test. Then as the horse became more confident in the transition to and from, I could diminish the steps into one step and have a clean transition from passage to piaffe within the same trot rhythm.

Gwen Blake

As in all levels of training, the transitions are the last thing to come. Piaffe-passage transitions are the ultimate strength-balance test for the horse.

Gary Rockwell

Being wide behind is a major fault in piaffe and passage. How do you correct it?

I put them on a circle and do four strides of passage to four strides of piaffe to four strides of passage and so on until the horse realizes that after four strides of passaging he's going to have to come right away and be balanced for a piaffe. After a while he realizes that the further out he gets his hind legs, the more difficult it is for him so he begins to keep his hind legs underneath him, knowing that one second later he'll come to the piaffe and it will be easier for him. Likewise, the horse that has problems going out to the passage is made more aware of his ability to retain his rhythm by the same exercise so he tends to find his way back to the passage easier and back to the piaffe easier. Usually this reduces slightly the size of a passage. The slight reduction of the size of the passage while maintaining very closed and engaged hind legs makes it easier for him to learn how to come through those transitions.

Robert Dover

Piaffe and passage make my horse tense. How can I keep him relaxed yet correct?

With a tense horse, I tend to ride him very deep. It might seem like a contradiction to ride a horse deep in one of the most collected movements that you can do, however, think about the fact that collection can be evaluated in terms of the relative height of the shoulders to the hindquarters. Thus you can have the neck and head of the horse quite low but if the shoulders are in a good spot, the horse is more collected than a horse whose head is high and whose shoulders are down. I tend to be able to keep a horse more relaxed riding him deep so I would do that. I would be sure to maintain a little bit of forward movement, perhaps gaining ground to the front, perhaps in the feeling of a pirouette. I try to avoid making the horse feel claustrophobic. I never want him to feel like 'I can't do this, I can't keep trotting,' and then he panics. The idea is to make it as simple for him as possible. I would do this in any other movement that I find particularly stress-producing. I also carry treats for something like that so that they associate it with pleasure. You can get rid of a lot of the tension that way.

Jane Savoie

Exercises you can use after the horse has learned piaffe and passage include shortening the passage, lengthening the passage, doing the piaffe with no aids at all and keeping the horse a little hot on your legs, but mostly short periods, very short periods of very perfect work.

Carol Grant Oldford

For the best piaffe/passage that I do with Zapatero I have to be totally focused, concentrating on his hind legs, not on my body at all. If I can hold the picture of his hind legs clearly in my mind's eye, and see his hind legs, see him bending his hocks — he does not miss a beat. As soon as my concentration wavers then I miss a step. Somehow my body is doing the right thing if my mind sees the correct picture. So I don't know what I'm doing. I don't know if it's something I'm doing with my seat. I don't know if it's something that I'm doing with my legs. I really don't know. I just know that if I can hold the picture of the perfect piaffe and passage in my mind, he does it. He's very sensitive. In fact, that's one of the reasons why I have to be sure not to give any aids. Because he's a sensitive horse, if I use my legs, he overreacts and stomps down too quickly. He's too fast with his hind legs and puts them on the ground too quickly so I have to be very clear either to not use my legs at all or to use them very softly and very, very lightly. If I give a quick aid, a sharp aid, a strong aid he overreacts by stomping down with a hind leg.

Jane Savoie

CHAPTER 12

Miscellany
(But Still Important)

Turnout is controversial, particularly with valuable horses. Do you turn yours out?

I think turnout is really, really important and I turn out all my horses. These horses are out all day which is different than most horses. I think they have to be allowed to be horses. Our paddocks are fairly small, but the pastures are huge and they stay in there a couple of hours a day. And when they're out every day, they don't really run. I know it's a risk but I think it's worth it. I don't think you can expect them to come out and be happy to work one hour a day when they've been standing staring at a wall all day. I just don't want to do that.

Charlotte Bredahl

Have you any advice on warming-up and cooling down?

During the warm-up I always work on basics. I usually start all the horse out long and low for the first ten minutes, and I also end up long and low with every horse for the last five minutes. This is even more important with the upper level ones because then you've done more contracting of the muscles and it's important to let them stretch at the end. After that, still as part of the warm-up, I usually start out with leg yields. Then I do lots of transitions — just basic transitions — walk-trot, lots of walk trot on any horse. Then trot canter, and then when they're warmed up, I do canter walks. I do lots and lots of transitions and lots of figure eights, serpentines and things like that. Then if everything is going well, I'll do movements but if things are not going really well, then I just do basics.

Another thing that I believe in is to have them cool down a long time. I know I do that a lot longer than most people. Luckily I have a groom — she'll hand walk Monsieur for one half hour every day after I ride him if he's worked hard. I think that makes a big difference in how they come out the next session.

                                                           Charlotte Bredahl

What other advice or comments would you share with riders?

I think a rider has to be very aware of accepting the individuality of each horse and not getting set on one technique and one program of training. I think the essence of a good trainer is the flexibility within their training concepts to allow the horse to be an individual, and to be able to bring out the best and preserve the individuality of each horse.

                                                             Belinda Nairn

Always to keep self-control, I think is very, very important. And that you shouldn't get angry when you're riding. And sometimes put yourself in the horse's place and make sure the horse is really understanding what you're asking. Try to make sure that your horse has as good a life as he can have, and then you can expect him to work when you take him out to work.

                                                           Charlotte Bredahl

One theme that keeps recurring in this discussion is the basic concept of riding the hindlegs forward to maintain balance and the purity of the gaits. In direct relation to this is the rider's ability to feel the hindlegs and ride the whole horse, not just what they see in front and feel in their hands. Riders of all levels need to be reminded of this and accept and seek outside input to achieve their goal of riding a balanced horse.

                                                              Ann Guptill

When I see competitions today, and I judge too, I believe that there are weaknesses in Second that are stemming from changes in the Second Level tests some years back to include collected and medium gaits. Originally working and lengthening were required. The idea was that the lower level horses in Europe really go forward, and they wanted to see our horses shoot forward in the trot and come back again. So they changed the test, yet we did not really change our judging. What was formerly judged sufficient in a lengthening became sufficient in a medium. I think we need to demand what is asked for in the tests. We're not doing the riders any favors by not demanding it because we're then not bridging the gap between the lower levels and the FEI classes. As a result, very often you see horses starting Prix St. Georges that have no collected balance. Top European judges seem to me to be more influenced by how the horse is working, and our judges have to begin to put more emphasis on that in the lower levels.

Many people in this country try to do the whole learning and training thing by themselves. Out country is so big and trainers are so spread out that there are many people who don't get regular help.

Top riders seem to have better and better access to top trainers today, largely thanks to USET programs. I hope that this straight-line European training will trickle down to middle-level riders and that beginners will then be able to make good use of their experience.

Gary Rockwell

I think it's vital to work with a trainer. I don't think you can do it without a trainer. Having been in Europe, I've seen that even the top trainers don't go to a show without a ground person. Don't let your ego get in the way of your development as a rider. Your horse will be the one to suffer for it.

Jane Savoie

I think every rider should think that it should be fun. It might be hard work at times but by gum, if you let your goals become too important, you get into trouble. But if you try to say to yourself, no matter how much pressure there may be on you to be great fast, it's very important to take your time and not lose sight of the fact that it should be fun.

Jessica Ransehousen

Don't buy a horse that's not suitable for the job at hand. You're stupid if you do. The job is hard enough. Don't buy breeding that's unsuitable either. There are certain breeds of horses that are not suited to this job, period. No matter what those breeding organizations say, look at the statistics and buy accordingly. There are line of Hanoverians that are not suited for dressage and the Germans know that. You can learn that easily. The same with other horses.

Carol Lavell

I think it's very important to be clear in the aids that are given the horse and to be firm but rewarding and never to use force.

Bent Jensen

There are no rules. No horse has ever read a book, and there are exceptions to everything that you hear or see or do. Whatever you read there's going to be one that does the exact opposite. And one is going to work and it's going to be just fine.

Pam Goodrich

I think if you can acquire a system of training and that you have a plan when you get on and you follow it each day, it keeps your horse very happy. And you can learn that from many good trainers and many good riders. You preserve the character of your horse and you work on your own position a lot. And I think perfect practice makes perfect work so you keep trying to do things well. I'd also like to say that I think beginning riders should really try to have experienced horses. I think if you're going to be a good rider you also have to learn that ability to train a little and you have to be able to relate to a horse and how he learns. I think some people never get that far and so they lose that ability to be really good riders.

Carol Grant Oldford

Listen to and observe your horse and he will teach you how to train him. What we call resistance is often a horse just expressing what he does not know yet. The clearer we are with our aids and in our riding, the sooner the horse will learn it. Take the time to learn the principles and system of classical dressage from the best trainers you can find. Always be patient. Exercise discipline and be firm when necessary, but never abusive. A horse like a child cannot defend himself — nor should he ever have to. Get help when you need it. Nobody knows everything. Keep your goal in sight — to help that horse to become the best that he can be — and enjoy the rewards of the process.

Kathy Connelly

When do you think a horse is ready to start showing?

The first couple of years I'm training a horse I really feel like we're playing with everything — it's sort of fun and if they do anything sort of right that's fine. And I don't usually show them very much. Maybe I should. I found with Monsieur that I ran into a lot of problems later, but I don't know that I wouldn't have anyway. I feel that once you start showing you get more demanding, and maybe you get too demanding. When I don't have the pressure of shows, I feel that I train better, especially the younger horses, because then you don't worry about everything being perfect. Not until you start showing do you say, "Okay, now I've got to be perfect." If you start to put that kind of pressure on a horse while he's still learning something, then it could take the fun out of it for the horse. They feel the pressure right away. So for the first couple of years I show very little. If I do take them out, I show them at a very low level so that there's no pressure.

Charlotte Bredahl

Horses vary in their timing for showing. The rider/trainer has to gauge how confirmed the horse's training is, how confident the horse is for presentation to the arena and what kind of temperament the horse has. Young horses are naturally more exuberant and can find it difficult to maintain a defined behavior within a 20 x 60 meter arena for six minutes when their minds are in fact swirling in firework explosions because of all of the outside stimuli. Often, the horses that turn out to be top horses later are like that. I don't show my own horses very much at the lower levels, but I give them exposure to shows by taking them with the show horses, riding them around the grounds and letting them absorb the scene. That way they get used to herds warming up together and strange looking judge's houses plopped unnaturally in the middle of sand areas, etc. Then when they actually show it is nothing special to them. Enterprise and Beethoven were both "feeling good" kinds of young horses and could potentially have produced unplanned excitement in their first shows. I spent a lot of time preparing them and they were both steady-Eddies in the ring after a few shows. I begin with my horses as young horses doing two riding seesions each day of the show. The first one just to hack out, relax and school a little. Then they are hand grazed and put back in the stall. That is the ride that defuses the bomb. Then the second ride is the warm up for the test. It takes the pressure off of them for the performance. I also do not usually show them while they are learning their most difficult things, because it is too much pressure for them to show then. But young horses are young horses, and it should not be a surprise nor cause for great dismay when the unplanned happens. It is an opportunity for the rider to evaluate the plan for tomorrow. There is always the next time.

Kathy Connelly

Can you give an approximate time table for a good rider to take a talented horse from Training to Fourth Level?

That really depends on the horse's mentality. Sometimes it can take, and it needs to take, a longer time because of the way the horse accepts the training. There are other horses who learn things very quickly and who are physically capable of moving along, and those horses can come along very quickly. Assuming you started the horse yourself as a three or four year old and you're not dealing with a horse with a different type of training or training problems — generally I would like to see a horse doing about Fourth Level sometime late in their six year old or seven year old year. Once a horse is a solid Fourth Level and has developed in the collection and the basic movements that are required at that level, then to go on from there becomes pretty easy. Having a proper basic foundation is the most important part of training, and I think it has to vary in accordance to what the horse will accept both physically and mentally.

Belinda Nairn

Every horse is different. You always have to let the horse tell you what to do. I would never set a time frame for my own horses. I never have. Sometimes you hope for something. I'm hoping I'll start my young horse in Prix St. Georges in the spring, but it's certainly not a matter of life and death. If he doesn't, it's just fine. It just depends on what he tells me he's ready for. But I would guess — First to Fourth Level — I would say two to three years.

Charlotte Bredahl

A general time table formula will not work for all horse and rider combinations. All riders of all abilities should have goals to work toward but each rider's and each horse's time tables are different depending on their abilities. Allowances have to be made for setbacks, too — whether due to training or illness or injury. Goals are good but different for each individual.

Ann Guptill

If that talented rider started with a three year old, and the three year old year is a difficult year, many times you have to get off because you can't control them. And I think it's better to get off before they know they're too strong. We have now a five year old we started at three. Sometimes even my good rider had to get off just because she wanted to be in control every moment out in the open field. You just make sure you don't get into a battle you can't get out of. A strong man maybe can get through the battle, but a woman, in my opinion, makes better horses because she has to teach the horse to be a good horse. So I would make sure that the horse always kept learning and never got into a battle even if you had to go around the bush to get through the front door. That would be the three year old year and they start at three years old to learn the turn on the forehand, to basically go forward and stop. Short periods of reward and punishment by asking again.

When they're four, they should already have developed a lengthening of trot, at least that they have the concept that when you put your legs on, they don't fall on their front end, they go forward. It might go forward maybe to canter, but they should start to have the concept at four of going forward and coming back easily and the concept of moving away from the leg but with a lot of rewards, because they're still not working partners yet. They still would rather not work six days. Also at four, they begin canter work. I always teach the canter from the walk in the beginning. When Lectron learned to canter, it was from walk first. And because he was the type, you could hit him and kick him and he'd run into the canter so we always taught it from the walk. And if they're not happy about that, if they don't want to go and they pin their ears back, then we send them briskly into trot. But we do teach the horse that he always has to be in front of the leg in a quiet way. Again, the nose is in front of the vertical, I would really keep stretching for that longer neck.

So I think if I had a really good rider we would go through the steps of teaching the horse leg-yielding, teaching him turn on the forehand, teaching him lengthening of stride with lots of reward. At this stage, one would start to be a little persistent, and if the horse starts to run in any gait, to make sure he knows suppleness and engagement in short periods.

At five I think they're ready for a good Second Level, because you put the pieces of the puzzle and you can ask more from them. But, in my opinion, transitions train the horse, so you might find some days he can't do medium canter to working canter but that he has to do canter trot work. You always have to go back steps when he has a problem. You go back to your foundation trot-canter/canter-walk.

At five they're starting their flying changes, but you never get angry if they make a mistake and you make them think it's fun. I keep encouraging my riders to make their young horses think it's still a game. And you do have the very talented ones that are a bit tense and nervous that you have to be careful that they don't think that your criticism is a punishment. If the training is going well, probably at six they can be doing (if they've had some show experience) Fourth Level. And then slowly you just keep putting the pieces to the puzzle together and your training is done. They've learned everything in the Grand Prix by the time they've finished even though they don't do everything in combination. Their concepts have been formed from three to six, and it's just a matter then of being able to go on, put the pieces together, do test riding, combinations — work on your own position, keep the horses happy and sound.

Carol Grant Oldford

If I were talking about perfect scenarios — a very talented rider and a very, very talented horse, then I would say to bring the horse along with absolutely classical basics. Never leave out one little bit of your basics and you'll find that by the age of five the horse is doing Second and some Third Level work and is also able to do a single flying change. By the time he is six he can do a lot of work from the Prix St. Georges and Intermediare One, and he can even have an idea about piaffe and passage. By the time he is seven he pretty much knows a lot of the Grand Prix work but he doesn't have to be doing the Grand Prix work. He can still be doing Prix St. Georges and Intermediare One. And by the time he is eight, the Grand Prix should be pretty much in that horse. Now that's a perfect scenario and then by the end of the eighth year into the ninth year you can be starting in the Grand Prix themselves, showing the Grand Prix. By ten, you should have a nice steady Grand Prix horse. So that is a perfect scenario but there's definitely nothing wrong with a horse who has very, very good basics by the time he is seven and then really is starting into a more formal education at seven, because, once again, by ten you can easily be doing Grand Prix. You must keep very steady in your desire to maintain classical basic principles. Once you have that, in a very talented horse everything is just waiting to come out.

Robert Dover

There is no such thing as a timetable. You can always hope that this year because there is an Olympic festival and next year because there's a North American Championship that you're going to have a horse ready. But in fact they do it when they're ready, you just have to stick to your training schedule and work the horse as it suits him as you go along. If you have a difficult horse, you may have to spend a lot of time on basics — relaxation and obedience, but then as you progress through the levels, they progress surprisingly fast. Or maybe with a horse that's not very talented you have to spend a lot of time trying to ride maximum gaits into the horse for some years and then when they achieve that, the advanced work comes very fast. Or on the other hand, maybe you have a horse that's been very easy in the lower levels and for whatever reason finds flying changes every stride exciting or passage or piaffe just physically difficult, you just have no choice. They're going to do it when they're going to do it.

Gary Rockwell

I think each horse makes his own timetable. The horse will tell you when things are difficult. And for the most part, resistance is something not to be afraid of. It is something you have to work through. As long as you follow a systematic program of development, resistance will be minor and temporary. Extreme resistance, however, might tell you that you have to plateau at some stage of training for a time until the horse gets mentally comfortable and physically strong enough at that level. So you might just blast through Training through Second Level, come to Third Level and plateau out for awhile. Horses are individuals so you have to listen to what the horse says to you by his struggles and by his resistance. Basically what you are doing when you're training him is developing a non-verbal language that you both understand — a vocabulary — one word at a time. You want to be very clear in your language in order to expedite training to whatever degree you can. You must be consistent. One's aids should always mean the same thing so that the horse does not have to play multiple choice. If the horse has to play multiple choice it's going to take you longer to train. You have to be consistent with your aids and consistent with your reinforcement. Your reinforcement is positive or negative depending on what the horse does. If you want a happy horse, basically your reinforcement should be reward rather than punishment. Understand that absence of reward is punishment and only occasionally do you need punishment more severe than that. If you give an aid and your horse gives you an appropriate response and you fail to reward him you've essentially punished him. As a result you're going to extinguish the behavior that you want to create. So keep in mind principles of behavior modification. You have a stimulus, an aid. Once the aid has been given and the horse responds, you must reinforce. Hopefully, a majority of your reinforcement will be positive and that is how you train your animal happily.

Jane Savoie

It's so individual. Some horses want to work harder and want to go on and some of them are really not sure. I don't know. It seems to me that every horse has his own timetable, and it's sometimes difficult to change it. I think you can get a horse doing movements but not really strong enough to do them well. I think on the whole if you wait for the body development and the muscle development, it's going to take awhile.

Jessica Ransehousen

The timetable is totally determined by the horse, not by the book that says all Third Level horses will be six years old, no older, otherwise it's too late for you, kid! Secondly, a talented horse can get stuck at a certain place and that's where he should stay until things are fixed. And sometimes he can get stuck at a certain place and you ignore that and you go right by it and do something else. For example, I have a six year old who is trying to learn to stay round and engaged in collected canter but I'm already doing and doing and doing it. He has a wonderful canter, but he is never on the straight line, and his quarters are never where I put them. He's always either falling forward on the bit or falling backwards away from the bit and he's never round. So I'm fixing those things the whole time. Now I could stay forever just cantering round and round the field, but it's going to take forever too. It's a possibility that exercises would actually improve this canter so I decided that the problem is that the hind legs need to be quicker and more under the horse's body. They could get quicker if I could teach him flying changes to make him answer the leg. The time when he's absolutely the best is when I'm doing random tempi changes. The quicker he is, the better he is. When Gifted was six he was doing a clean flying change to the left and a late one to the right. I'm only working on ones with this young horse because he has a wonderful canter and Gifted did not. With a couple of horses I've started things too early, and I paid for it dearly. And so now I know there are certain things I shouldn't start too early but I always start the piaffe early but only half steps. And I have someone walk along side the horse with the whip to get him used to that. That starts early so that he gets accustomed to it and it's like stepping out of bed in the morning.

The timetable in the beginning is crucial. I've tried breaking three year olds and working them and I don't get anything out of them. I'm just wasting my time riding around. And I've heard the story that they are getting bigger and stronger and I've got to break them now. No. If they're getting bigger and stronger they're also getting hurt when they're three. You have to lunge them and that can be a problem. I never lunged Gifted because he was too big. The difficulty is that you can hurt a big horse very badly on the lunge. To play on the lunge is the worst thing that can happen to a big horse. He can just land wrong and break something. You have to toss out certain things in the book that say you have to do this at a certain time in the horse's training. However, in the beginning, there are some things the timetable determines: obedience to the hand and leg, loading in the trailer. The horse is being tamed. Those things must be in place or you're in trouble. So I start almost all of them at four unless I have to break a three year old because I'm going away and I don't want to come back when he's four and three-quarters and break him. I break them in October, November and turn them out for the winter and bring them back in May. At the four year old year the whole time is spent steering and going forward, that's all. By the end of the four year old year, they've gone outside, they've gone trail riding, they've been in the trailer, they've been in different stalls, they know what a bath is all about, they know what a farrier is, they all know about vaccinations, they know a whole lot actually more than you think they do. And they have to go where I say. They don't have to go straight but they have to go where I say. The timetable says that at four years old when you put the leg on the horse, there's only one thing that this horse has got to do. The leg and the whip mean forward and I promise not to pull on the reins at the same time. And if he doesn't understand that at four, I dare you to impress the five year old that's big and strong with this without getting in trouble.

At five, it's much more serious unless we have unfortunate problems like a giant four year old turning five who has to grow up more in which case I just leave him and let him grow up. Gifted was like that — could barely work. The rest of my horses, smaller ones, are working hard. What are they working at? The bit is mine. They don't have to be perfectly straight, but the bit is mine. Don't lean on it, don't push on it, don't lock your poll, don't lock you jaw. I'm taking it away and then pushing them forward. At this stage they're not on the bit — they're just against it or fooling around a lot, crooked, not forward — stuff like that and I'm correcting that. All we're doing is walk, trot and canter, a little bit of leg yield, some shoulder-fore stuff and some transitions. You're not doing half-pass, I'm not really doing shoulder-in (I used to do shoulder-in at this point, but I learned better). It's not the right thing to do yet. I can put them in the bend and the angle, but I'm creating crookedness, I'm creating lack of forwardness. Don't start doing that. The five year old year can actually be kind of boring but it's a very important year. This is the year where the horse might have some very strong things to say about how much work he wants to do. He might think this is a lot of work when in truth if he knew what his future held, it's not a lot of work at all. I've seen people take five year olds and fool around teaching them piaffe steps. I've done that too, but I actually wasted my time, because the big thing that I needed to spend by time was on going forward, turning, and bending. It doesn't have to be perfect, but when I say look right, or look left, I mean it. The horse's body is beginning to belong to me. We're just getting the body to be manipulated. If you let too much time escape past five, you won't get that. You're just going to get an argument and it's going to be serious.

By the age of six he should have already two years of strong basic training. If you have to start them at six, you've got a mature horse now, many a six year old is not easy to impress. It could already be too late. If at the end of the five year old year, you're still trying to establish who's boss, you've got troubles. Many good horses have had that problem right up to age six and seven — who's the boss here? Ahlerich was one of them. He was constantly bucking Klimke off, constantly taking charge, leaving the ring, taking off with him, doing horrible things to him. So it is true we have exceptions to this rule, but for us novice riders working with our plain, ordinary backyard horse, these things need to be done early or it could be down to a matter of survival.

Seven years old ideally I'd like them to be Third and Fourth Level and Prix St. Georges if they're really talented. At eight years old I like to start thinking about Prix St. Georges. Now I want Fourth and Prix St. Georges. Nine years old it sure would be nice to see higher than Prix St. Georges.

Gifted was six at Third Level. That's all he could do was Third Level. He could not do anything else but that. And at seven year old I went Fourth Level and Prix St. Georges "over Mike's dead body." He was sure I couldn't do it. At eight years old he went Prix St. Georges and Intermediare. I did one Intermediare II test only when he was eight and started Grand Prix at nine. But he was an exceptional horse.

Now it's 1994, and we have been in Grand Prix since 1989. We're entering our sixth season and embarking on our fifth European tour. I feel we have just become really competent at most of the movements, and I now have a clear idea of how much collection is needed to do these well versus going through the motions performing a collection of "tricks." Our everyday work consists of basic training for collection and throughness — no rehearsals of the movements until two weeks before competition. It was very hard for me to learn that Gifted could do all the things very well and needed no practice if he was through. I turned out to be the one who needed practice!

Carol Lavell

Who were your major influences as a rider or trainer?

Bengt Ljunquist was probably my greatest inspiration. I came to him at the age of 13 and stayed with him until he died. From him, I learned a lot more than just dressage riding. I learned a love for horses and a love for harmony and beauty in dressage, and also I learned about honor and justice from Bengt Ljunquist. There is something to be said for somebody who comes from that kind of background which was the Swedish cavalry. He had been a five-time fencing Olympian as well as a one-time dressage Olympian. He knew how dressage related to the rest of life, and I learned I think a lot about life beyond horses from him.

After he died, I had the opportunity to train with people like Willi Schultheis, George Theodorescu, Herbert Rehbein, and Harry Boldt. I found all of them to be, in their own right, very, very artistic, very loving of the horses, and I learned something from every one of them. It wasn't always positive things that I learned but I made them into positive things. If I thought there was something negative about something I had learned then I would try to turn that around into remembering never to do it a certain way and always to do it another way.

Robert Dover

I'm not training with anyone now. I trained with Rehbein in Europe. This year I was only there for six weeks but last year I was there for four months. That was very good, it was very good to be in a place with so many good horses and riders because I'd been off on my own for so many years hoping that I was doing the right thing, but not really knowing. Just being in a place where you see nothing but Grand Prix horses is really wonderful. Hilda Gurney has helped me over the years — she helped me quite a bit with my first Grand Prix on the horse Copenhagen when I first started training him. I've also taken lessons from different people in clinic. I took some from Harry Boldt and I think he's fantastic. We took some with him this year and some last year and I've taken clinics with Christine Stuckelberger. I have ridden with Robert Dover quite a bit.

Charlotte Bredahl

My first introduction to upper level dressage was with Nuno Oliveira. He was a master at training horses to do the movements.

Michael Poulin taught me how to ride. I could train the movements, but I couldn't ride even the basic walk, trot, or canter correctly. He taught me to ride while continuing my training.

Herbert Rehbein has helped me a lot to engage and develop more collection and self carriage. As a German, he polished and improved the quality of the work. He is unique in his ability to adjust to the different styles of horses.

Harry Boldt is another one that has helped me to polish the performance. He is exceptionally good at how to ride the test. He has an excellent eye and can make slight adjustments that improve the movement.

Lendon Gray has helped me a lot to make the difference between training and competing. She helped me to train at home and then let the horse perform, so when competing it comes out as a smooth polished performance.

Carol Lavell has been a great help. She is very particular that the horse does things just right. She has a keen eye and encourages the rider to ride for perfection.

Pam Goodrich

I was fortunate as a child, starting at nine years old, to grow up in the Glastonbury Pony Club, where our leader Jan Conant, regularly invited for clinics the current U.S. Team riders to teach us. Among them were George Morris and Jessica Ransehousen. They were very patient with us, and tremendous educators.

Over the years, in the United States, I have benefited greatly from the generous help of Cindy Sydnor and Jessica Ransehousen. Each with a different approach and great dedication. I have worked also with Robert Dover, who has an exceptional eye and an ability to articulate the picture, in addition to being a very gifted rider. I learned a great deal about the way to ride a Grand Prix test from Harry

Boldt. I really enjoyed working with him. Michael Poulin is a master at training piaffe and passage and has particular brilliance at communicating this talent. He has been extremely helpful to me and very generous.

I have had the good fortune to train in Austria with Ernst Bachinger from the Spanish Riding School of Vienna. Bachinger is a genius magician with long lines and work in hand. He has a deep love of horses and is a beautiful rider. He knows how to do less to get more from a horse, and he does it easily.

I have trained with Herbert Rehbein in Germany with both Enterprise and Beethoven. I believe him to be not only one of the best riders in the world, but one of the best riders in the history of the world. Both of these horses were sensitive. Rehbein was always firm but gentle — never too strong. His understanding and love of the horse emanate from his riding — he really knows how a horse thinks. He is a master at preparing a horse for Grand Prix competition. Both Bachinger and Rehbein know how to keep the magic in a horse and are truly inspirational.

Kathy Connelly

I started out wanting to do something serious with dressage in about 1969. I had only been around it for just a little over a year, but I somehow realized that it was necessary to do some kind of a long-term program. At that time in this country there was little direction available, very few dressage trainers, no USDF, no directory of trainers. You had to find your way yourself just by having seen someone ride or by word of mouth. I went to Lilian Wittmack-Roye in York, Pennsylvania. She was an international jumping rider from Denmark, who, of course, also had extensive dressage training. She came to the U.S. in the 50's and was our national dressage champion several times. I apprenticed with her for a little over five years and got a very good foundation. She had a very, very good eye for horses and for riding position and the effect of the aids. Most of all, she was an incomparable horsewoman — there was nothing she hadn't done or couldn't do with a horse. With her I began to develop a real love and feeling toward horses — not to mention horse sense. I then worked for many years pretty much on my own. I worked whenever possible with Gunnar Ostergaard who was very helpful, then later with Jorgen Olsen in Denmark. His quiet training technique was familiar and attractive, and over a period of ten years he was an enormous help in developing my riding and my eye. In 1991, I went to Robert Dover for help in finishing my mare, Suna. I very much admire his ability and his approach to the training of the horse — the constant awareness of how the rider affects the horse and how to make them work together.

Gary Rockwell

Which partnership with a horse was your most memorable?

I learned so much from each one that it would be hard to even put into words what I learned. From Romantico, who had such a wonderful temperament but who was, to some degree, short on natural talents in the canter work, I learned how to make the best of a situation that wasn't perfect. I kept on learning that same lesson with the next horses because there is no such thing as a perfect horse. What you have to do is believe in your ability with that horse to achieve your goal and then to make him the best horse that he can possibly be. So from Federleit, who was a horse that I more than just cared about as a dressage horse but also loved like a pet and had ever since he was a young horse, I learned how to take an animal that was very hot in the beginning and make him into a reliable Olympic mount. From Juvel I learned how to maintain patience and also to bring a horse who didn't have always perfectly engaged hind legs to looking like he could go through the entire Grand Prix with a great degree of ease. With Waltzertakt again I learned patience and that you had to train a horse that was very, very hot to be reliable through the use of warming up, possibly twice, or once in the morning and then once for your ride. I've learned from all the horses I've dealt with, whether they were my horses or other people's horses, a lot about dressage riding and a lot about the rest of life as well.

Robert Dover

For me the easiest horse has been Gifted. You ask Mike Poulin and he'll tell you that he was one of my most difficult horses. Gabby Grillo, Michael Poulin, Harry Boldt and Herbert Rehbein will all tell you that Gifted is an extraordinarily difficult horse to ride. To me he is the easiest horse I have ever ridden in my life. It could be because I cut my teeth on Polish Trakehners: Lilak, Symbol, In the Black. They were difficult, because they were the horses I was also learning on so I didn't make their life any easier either. Lilak was my first Grand Prix horse. He was easy to train, but he had physical limitations. Before him I had a different horse I had to teach flying changes to. He had terrible canter, and I had to learn how to teach flying changes to a horse who was just totally untalented in flying changes and then he turned out to be good at them. Then when it came to Lilak, he couldn't canter either but at least I knew how to fix it. After I made the canter better, the flying changes were a piece of cake. It really put it home to me that you had to have a good enough canter before you started flying changes.

The most difficult horse in the world mentally was In the Black, because he never wanted to work. I finally got him to Grand Prix and then I gave up because I was just sick and tired of forcing the work out of the horse. He just didn't want to work. He had a bad attitude and no idea about work. But he was a talented horse, and he could do things. I could do one and one half Grand Prix zig-zags in the ring because he was so good at them. And I can just barely get a half of one on Gifted if I'm lucky. In the Black could do flying changes until the cows came home and he could do a pirouette any place at any time and any number of them on the centerline — right, left, left right — anytime — all perfect. He was so talented, but just difficult in the brain. Lilak had a wonderful brain but a difficult body to teach. Always an honest horse, always trying. Symbol was a stallion, and I didn't know anything about necks and jaws. Mike said he had a bad neck and jaw, and I didn't even know what he meant. He said I'd need a draw rein to fix that, because he was way too strong for me. I didn't have any. What I learned from that horse! Symbol was the only horse I've ever owned who entering Fourth Level never got a score below 70 percent. Gifted never did that. Symbol was unreal, he was so good. But difficult. So much more difficult to ride than Gifted. Certainly Gifted has given me the most vivid moments — from the day I first put the saddle on to the day I took it off after his Barcelona Olympic Games bronze medal ride it has been some trip!

Carol Lavell

Each horse begins a new story, and is a new process of learning. My first Grand Prix horse, I bought all trained so I could learn from him. His name was Puchacay — an import from Chile, an older horse when I got him. He was noble and had a super piaffe and passage. He had learned it on the long lines.

Gabrielle was a very elegant horse — extremely sensitive and an overachiever. She was a hot horse and had all of the inherent characteristics of a Thoroughbred. I learned so much about showing from her. She was claustrophobic about going into show arenas. Eventually, she overcame her fear, and was very steady in the arena. From her I learned great patience, and how to prepare difficult horses to show. Nothing could ever be forced.

Enterprise, my Danish Grand Prix horse, was a delight to train, because he was sensitive and forward thinking. Canter pirouettes and the zig-zags were his most difficult movements to learn. The flying changes, piaffe and passage, he learned easily. He was an exuberant horse, which held him in good stead when the show conditions were difficult — hot weather or whatever. He always had lots of energy and was extremely reliable in the competitive arena.

Beethoven, my Dutch horse, was born with abundant enthusiasm and a high self esteem. He is a very intelligent horse and learned quickly. He is the horse I have had to think the most with in the training, because he was so bright and could have learned things incorrectly as quickly as correctly. I spent an extra amount of time on basics with him, so that his foundation would be very strong. The movements were very easy for him to learn, especially the piaffe-passage for which he has an extraordinary natural gift. I prepared him carefully for the show arena, exposing him to lot of experiences before showing him. He has been my easiest horse to introduce to the show arena. He is extra special fun because he loves to perform and has a lot of presence.

I have found each of my horses to be a tremendously gratifying and humbling experience. Gratifying, because they were so rewarding. Humbling, because they were so generous in their hearts, in the way that a horse can be. Not just in day to day training, but when the chips were down, in competition. I have learned so much from them.

Kathy Connelly

With Forstrat it was interesting, because I really trained almost full time. First, with a trainer we went with Liselotte Linsehoff and then with Gunnar Andersen. So a lot of the training of that horse was more or less just doing what everybody else said I should do. Keeping him once he was there was not so hard, and then the second Olympics was more just keeping him going and perfecting the movements and so on. With Orpheus it was different. Orphy was a lot of fun, but he was a little bit difficult in some areas. He was always a challenge and a lot of fun to ride, and I really could use the timetable that I felt was right with him by then and I didn't have to sacrifice what I thought would be important in getting him ready.

Jessica Ransehousen

When he was learning his changes, Ben was hysterical. He closed his eyes and he flung himself left and right with his front end. And when I say fling, I mean he needed the whole arena. It took him a year to figure out how to do a quiet single change. Once he figured out how to do a quiet single change, the four, three, and two tempis were a piece of cake. Then I went to do one-tempis and he was bonkers. He was so worried and tense that he dove his shoulders left and right. I finally was able to half-halt his head up as he did each change. Then he figured out to keep his head up instead of diving on his shoulders. He's such a trier that he held himself up — no contact — and did some. This is when he opened his eyes and understood. They are really good now.

Adriano was very difficult in one-tempis. His problem was that he didn't have a big enough canter. He had no suspension. Plus he is half Thoroughbred and the quickness of the aids made him very nervous. For the first year I showed him Intermediare II and Grand Prix, he had only one line of one-tempis. If I practiced them, he got more and more nervous and they were not good. So, I competed him without practicing in the warm-up. I could trust him to do the one line. He always did. After a year, he relaxed enough to be able to do several lines and remain calm.

Pam Goodrich

How important do you think it is for serious American riders to get training in Europe?

I think it's very important, but they don't have to get the basic training there. They won't get as good basic training there as they will here in the States. But when it comes to the hard stuff, the Grand Prix, the FEI in general, they need to go over there or have help from people who have trained over there. You get more honest help here — people who are going to take the time to teach you whatever is necessary to teach you. You don't get that over there. You may, but you've got to be careful about it and therefore that's why you should have a pretty sound base before you do go over there.

Pam Goodrich

I think when their ability in the States is good enough, of course they should go to Europe and look at the total picture and be taught by Europeans. I think there are so many good instructors in America to take them to that point. I think if they're sent there too early, the Europeans don't do as much baby-sitting and good teaching possibly — oh, they do it and you learn it by osmosis, but in America we can't quite do that and so we have teachers who do spend the time teaching. And then once you know it, I think it's good to go there.

Carol Grant Oldford